# *Donald English*

# FROM
# WESLEY'S
# CHAIR

*Presidential Addresses*

*London*
**EPWORTH PRESS**

*Enquiries should be addressed to*
*The Methodist Publishing House*
*Wellington Road*
*Wimbledon*
*London SW19 8EU*
*Printed in Great Britain by*
*The Garden City Press Limited*
*Letchworth, Hertfordshire SG6 1JS*

# FROM WESLEY'S CHAIR

*To Robert and Ena English*

# CONTENTS

# PREFACE

THE itinerary of a Methodist President is not organized to facilitate the writing of a book! This one has been possible because its content is derived from addresses given on various occasions. Yet they are not verbatim accounts of the talks given. They are in written form intended for readers, not spoken form prepared for hearers.

As one whose task is to teach Theology, I have tried to work from a theological base in each chapter. And since my particular fields are Practical Theology and Methodism these areas have naturally influenced the direction of thought. My hope is that readers will be encouraged to explore various issues of Christian belief in such a way as to relate them to the practical business of living the Christian life today. Groups could well use the material as a basis for discussion.

My debt to my wife, Bertha, and sons Richard and Paul, during this heavy year is incalculable. I am also deeply grateful to those who have so faithfully supported me in prayer, and I am glad to take this opportunity to express my thanks, with great admiration, to the Methodist people. They have made this an unforgettable year for me.

The Editor of the Epworth Press, the Rev. John Stacey, has facilitated the production of this book with characteristic patience and graciousness. To him I owe the suggestion of the title. I wish also to thank the General Manager of the Methodist Publishing House, Mr Albert Jakeway, and his staff for the speed with which this book has been produced. Mrs Hilary James has typed the manuscripts with great cheerfulness and efficiency, and I am most grateful to her.

## FROM WESLEY'S CHAIR

I become increasingly convinced that the Church needs a deeper grasp of theological understanding and clearer insights into the way in which it will relate to daily life. I hope this book may be of some use to those who share that concern.

DONALD ENGLISH

# I

## CHURCH

CHAPTER ONE

# Hope

*Presidential Address, The Methodist Conference,*
*Eastbrook Hall, Bradford*
*23 June 1978*

A RECENT television programme, 'Horizon', was about the development of computerization. It included the comment 'It all depends on whether our nation can learn to live meaningful lives'. The unlikelihood of our learning to do so was depressingly illustrated by the alternative choice of programme at that time. It was organized by 'Women against Rape'. That illustration may set the mood and remind us of the sombre circumstances in which we meet as a Conference.

This very city of Bradford has recently published a report forecasting increasing problems for itself as the black population grows, the white population decreases, investment in industry drops and the jobs become fewer and fewer, with black people likely to lose out.

Not long before that some Cambridge economists wrote of the possible figure of five million unemployed by the end of the century. Other projections on unemployment warn particularly of the danger of a large band between the ages of sixteen and twenty-five who will be out of work, with all the dangerous political and social implications of such a situation. Not all agree about the various projections, and immediate current trends show some signs of improvement, but this will be of greater encouragement to the Government than to the one and a half million out of work at present.

The world picture seems little better. There is greater complexity, larger threat, increased misery. The names of Steve Biko and Aldo Moro, at different ends of the spectrum, are reminders of the nature of things. For those two whose names we know, how many un-named persons suffer unknown? Alongside this we must place the estimate that only 27 per cent of the world's population is Christian, a constant rebuke to our lack of missionary concern. And there are the 700 million people who exist on less than 10p a day each, who are a constant rebuke to our lack of human compassion.

In such a setting it would be heartening to speak of a church strong and ready for action. Yet our ministerial stations will include this year gaps which mean cutting back to the live wood of the tree. Our financial situation reflects inability to meet needs and to take up opportunities because of limited resources. Our communication and contact with whole areas of society is weak or non-existent. *The thought of the church becoming a trend-setter in our culture, as opposed to being a trend-chaser, is almost an exquisite form of self-torture.*

We have faced an unprecedented rate of change in lifestyle, social structures, political development, available knowledge, the multiplicity of sub-cultures, wide travel and communication, and concepts of freedom and individuality. My parents have probably lived through an era whose rate and extent of change is as great as all previous centuries of recorded history put together. No wonder we have found it difficult to respond adequately and effectively at all points.

Yet the Christian Church ought not to be too despondent about her responses to such change. *In the area of doctrine* our thinking in the '60s cut back to the heart and bone of the faith.

Some would say we were set fair to amputate both! It was a form of self-inflicted pain of a very impressive kind. Maybe we *did* set a trend there. Perhaps it is also good that we recovered after such severe surgery to find that we were not as ill as we had thought! The exploration continues and although the scalpels have been out again recently, for many it has become a much more positive and satisfying search than it was in the '60s.

*Concerning worship,* liturgical groups (and some very non-liturgical groups) have influenced our practice quite significantly. Had I, in my days as Assistant Tutor at Wesley College, Headingley, been hugged by a young lady in the context of worship as I was recently at Wesley College, Bristol, I would have thought it, however enjoyable, to be highly improper! Things are undoubtedly changing. The wide use of the 'Sunday Service' in an indication here, though not in the direction of 'holy huggery'.

*In our organization* it might be something of an exaggeration to say that all Methodists are totally satisfied with our new structures. (I am greatly relieved that the debate comes up at the next Conference and not this!) But we have attempted it in the interests of more effective church life and growth and that is a point of some significance.

*In the matter of resources* the past twenty years in particular have forced us to review our situation; whether by *stewardship,* through wider considerations of *ministry* (even though not all are enamoured of the suggestions or developments and the debate continues), or through the inspiring lead given us by the *Church Membership Committee,* whose results are available for us.

Alongside these more formal and institutional elements, we may note also some developments which have broken through the surface of church life, so to speak, rather than having been created through the structures. There is the vast increase of Christian concern to help the needy—physically, socially and politically. There is the personal and corporate renewal enjoyed by many Christians through forms of charismatic experience. There is a growing confidence about proclaiming the Christian good news. There is the increasing improvement at informal levels of relationships between Christians. I hope tomorrow night's Ecumenical Service will celebrate such improvement, World Cup tie notwithstanding. There are the large numbers of young people who still look to us for guidance and leadership, almost 130,000 over the age of fourteen and who receive it, as the recent MAYC weekend again demonstrated, very movingly.

So there is a great deal for which to be thankful and to make us consider a moratorium on 'church-bashing by church-goers'. The danger is that in following this latest popular Christian sport we may be found opposing the Holy Spirit. We have lots of good and moving stories to tell. Why do we not tell them? Decay and decline are *not* inevitable elements in Christian church life. Why do we behave as though they were? The Christian gospel *can* spread, the church *can* grow, and God *can* be more honoured in our land. Maybe the Church Growth Movement and the Nationwide Initiative in Evangelism will help us here. I hope to share and discuss the insights of such developments in my visits to the Districts. Some of the signs are there in this review. *Have we become so good at recognizing rain-clouds that we have lost the art of discerning the rising of the sun?*

The invitation I wish to make is in no sense an alternative to the realistic responses outlined so far. It is rather to examine the soil in which their roots are set. Certainly one wishes to ensure that the roots *are* set there, but one also wishes to discover how the roots may draw fully on the sustenance available.

If we require a text it would be taken from the Psalm out of which God spoke to John Wesley on 24 May 1738, the day of the Aldersgate Street experience. In the afternoon at St Paul's he heard the anthem based on Psalm 130, including the words 'O Israel, hope in the Lord'. The combination of this with the earlier reading of 2 Peter 1:4 on claiming God's promises,* and the later listening to Luther's preface to Romans, on God's work in the life of the individual, provided the stimulus for the warmed heart. The catalyst for the Methodist revival was Wesley's understanding of what it meant to 'Hope in the Lord'. My invitation is for us to explore that in our setting today.

First, *to hope in the Lord involves a theological task.* If our hope *is* in the Lord, or, as another Psalm puts it 'the Lord *is* our hope', then we cannot avoid asking 'who is the Lord?' This is a theological question. Theology is strictly speaking 'the science of God', as N. P. Williams described it years ago. Or it is, as E. L. Mascall has more recently put it, 'A study of God, and of God's creatures in relation to him'. The order of that definition is important; God first and our relationship to him second.

Basically, theology is an exploration in response to a reve- lation; a search amongst the evidence God himself discloses. Moreover it is a search best undertaken on one's knees, in awe and reverence; though with the mind fully engaged. It is a pilgrimage to the heart of reality which for the Christian begins in Jesus Christ and ends by calling his Father our Father.

In practice it means, as we evolve our responses in a chang- ing world, that we ask not only 'does it work?' but 'is it true?'; not only 'is it impressive?' but 'is it authentic?'; not only 'is it modern?' but 'is it Christian?'; and not only 'is it a relevant lifestyle?' but 'does it truly reveal God?' Maybe we would make the search and its implications clearer if we ceased talking about a theology *of* mission, theology *of* worship, theology *of* the church, theology *of* liberation, and began replacing the 'of' with an 'and'. 'Theology *and* mission' would

---

* 'God has granted to us his precious and very great promises, that through these we may escape from the corruption that is in the world because of passion, and become partakers of the divine nature.'

force us to ask how far our mission is actually a participation in God's one mission to his world. 'Theology *and* worship' would require us to ask whether the worship we bring is appropriate to the nature of the God to whom it is offered. 'Theology *and* liberation' would raise the question of whether the liberation we offer is the kind that the Christian God actually makes available in his world. What would our mid-week programme cards communicate to a total stranger about our basic purpose and reason for existence? This way we would force our search back to the first point of every exploration, the nature and purpose of God himself. Then we would at least know that our 'hope' *was* 'in the Lord'.

Secondly, *hope has a past, a present and a future.* Many of us are familiar with the problem of bi-focalization in spectacles. The Christian's task is an even greater one. It requires tri-focalization, the ability in this case to look in three different directions at once.

There is ground for hope in our past, in God's self-revelation in history, and particularly in the life, death and resurrection of Jesus. He is the paradigm for our understanding, the pattern for our action, the basic story which gives meaning to all our stories. A church which loses its memory about this basic foundation of hope is as pitiful as the individual who loses his memory in everyday life. The onset of fantasy and delusion is never far away. We test our vision and our hope by the foundational picture of God in Christ. We cannot avoid the constant task of teaching the faith, telling the story, recounting our beginnings.

But hope in the Lord cannot be entirely restricted to the past, otherwise we can replace our churches by museums, our membership lists by catalogues of relics, our worship services by exhibition hours. The Jesus of history is to be known as the Christ of faith, not only alive then, but alive now and known to his people. The testimonies of those newly come to the faith are a constant reminder of the essential link between past and present as grounds of hope. As Paul put it to the

Philippians, 'I press on to make it (full salvation) my own because Christ Jesus has made me his own' (Philippians 3:12). The aim of the teaching is that people might not only learn about Christ but come to know him for themselves. What many of our churches lack is the new life brought by converts from right outside, with all the splendid freshness of the uninitiated.

And hope has a future. The evidence of the past and the experience of the present provide the basis for hope in the future. The risk is a genuine one, and it is a total one. Like Abraham, according to the writer to the Hebrews, we do not know where we will be going. But as one commentator remarked about Abraham in that passage, 'we know *with whom* we are going'. To quote Wesley, 'the best of all is, God is with us'. Do we betray our lack of faith by our unwillingness to risk ourselves in the interests of others? Assurance of present salvation was never intended to partner caution in outreach.

In the third place, *hope in the Lord is undeterred by circumstances*. There is enormous pressure upon us today to demonstrate our relevance as a church. The pressure is highest when it comes from within ourselves, when *we* feel that Christianity stands or falls by its contemporary value and demonstrable usefulness. None of us wishes to be regarded as a back-number and one of the most demoralizing criticisms of the church today is that it is simply 'out of date'.

The easiest (and often an effective) response is the pragmatic one. We begin to collect evidence. We produce graphs which demonstrate trends. We take the realistic action needed to correct the trends. We re-allocate our resources, we cut our losses, we project for the future, and often the downward trend continues.

To avoid misunderstanding, let me say again that this is not to criticize any of these responses in themselves. Too often the church has neglected, criminally, to collect, evaluate and act upon available data. Hoping in God is no alternative to proper expertise and careful planning. As our vision of God is daily renewed we still need all the skills and organization of which we are capable as we seek to reflect his nature in our words and actions.

The invidious part of the process. however, is that by which we come to put our trust in our ability to respond realistically to the current situation. Our giving is then measured by our ability to meet the budget; our worship by the number attending; our ministry by the amount of activity it produces; our effectiveness in the world by the number of statements we make on political, social and economic matters.

But the hope of the church never did rest in these things. The heart of the gospel is that we are justified by grace through faith, not by performance through success, and even that faith is a response to divine initiative. *The justification of the church is its Lord, not its achievements.* The effectiveness of its life is measured by its faithfulness, not its success. Its value in the world is judged, not by the quantity of its actions or words but by the degree to which both words and actions provide signposts to the reality of God's presence in the world and to the nature and purposes of that God. Then giving will be measured, not by the budget, but by the openhearted response of God's people in gratitude. Worship will be judged by the extent to which we sense the presence of God, offer ourselves wholly to him and are equipped again to discern his presence in daily life and to serve him there. Ministry will be tested by the degree to which God uses it to bring others to faith, to build up the church, to serve the world. Our effectiveness will be assessed by our true portrayal of God's love to the world and by setting people free to love and serve him.

If I read my Bible aright on this point, *the way forward* out of times of difficulty and depression has been found by individuals or groups who, in the darkest days, *were brought back* to the source of hope—the Lord himself. Abraham and his call, Moses and the burning bush, Isaiah in the temple, Ezekiel with his vision, John the Baptist in his solitude and

Paul on the Damascus Road are all shadows of the one true man, Jesus Christ, who constantly faced the pressing challenges of his ministry by reflecting upon and communing with his heavenly Father. They faced their circumstances realistically but they did not find there the resource to deal with them. With their vision of God renewed, circumstances of any kind could be faced with hope, for their hope was not in the circumstances nor in successfully facing them. Their hope was in the Lord. Is this the message our own people are delivering to us in their increasing request for Bible Study and teaching on the content of the faith? They have been exhorted again and again to perform a variety of actions as Christians. Do they now want to test that beneath the actions there is a justification in the life of God himself?

In the fourth place, *hope in the Lord gives us a necessary freedom within our cultural setting.* No one will doubt the necessity of accepting our place within our own culture and its many sub-cultures. We cannot return to a former age, or live as though our cultural setting were different from what it is. Nor do we believe that God is somehow locked up in some previous culture, whether the first or the eighteenth or any other century. We believe him to be active in our culture. Nor is the Christian's relation to his cultural setting an easy one to evaluate, despite the help given by Tillich, Niebuhr and others.

One thing is clear, however, and that is the danger of Christians separately and the Church corporately becoming encased within a culture so effectively that the standards, attitudes and practices of the culture become the norm for Christians, even when they are contrary to a truly Christian life-style. We become acclimatized within our setting, failing to see its contours clearly till, in the end, the Christian is no different from any other person.

It is hope in the Lord which renews our vision of a just society when life around us denies its chances. It is hope in the Lord which sharpens our perception of spiritual realities midst a society where materialism is rampant. It is hope in the Lord which strengthens us to fight for lost causes and needy peoples because God's bias is towards the lost and the needy, even when we lose reputation and status because of the struggle. It is hope in the Lord which keeps us on Christian course even when we are essentially a minority—sometimes of one—in our own setting. It is that hope which enabled three Hebrews, faced by the threat of a fiery furnace, still to refuse to bow down to the image of the king, simply because it was not appropriate for those who served their God (Daniel 3). And it is hope in the Lord which will enable us to perceive his presence even in the complexity of modern life, because, primarily, in the complexity of Jesus' life and death God involved himself for our salvation.

Fifthly, *hope in the Lord speaks to the desolate too*. Hope is so often linked to starry-eyed idealism that one who hopes is treated as naïve or unrealistic. Or hope is viewed as a shallow response to deep problems. The Christian hope should never be capable of such criticism. The Lord is its source, and he revealed himself supremely in Jesus Christ. The climax of hope was Christ's willingness to go to the cross. He hoped in God as he gave up his life. The resurrection confirmed the accuracy of such hope. And the death and resurrection of Jesus became the ground of hope for all who would believe.

The Christian hope is therefore movingly relevant to the oppressed and the sorrowful, for it is planted at the foot of the cross, with resurrection promise. The Jesus who is at the centre of our hope is one who knows more deeply than any man the depths of pain, desolation and rejection. Hope begins there, and the death and resurrection pattern is the clue to its outworking. As South African Methodist minister, Stanley Mogoba, put it 'Oppression draws its strength from its acceptance in the mind of the oppressed'. Only a hope which meets a person at the point of oppression, degradation, desolation and loneliness will do. At the foot of the cross, the Christian hope is able to do precisely that. My question is whether we are open enough and near enough to people outside the church to tread with awe over the soil of their lives where the Cross which meets their desolation can be planted. And is the effective centre of our lives the soil where the cross is implanted and resurrection a daily occurrence?

Sixthly, *hope in the Lord unites word and action, proclamation and presence.* One trusts that we are nearing the end of the battle between Christian activists and proclaimers, between social workers and evangelists.

Maybe we can hasten the cessation of hostilities by issuing a call to all Christians to *unite in sending up signals of hope.* Most actions require interpretation; most interpretations require a setting in action. In our search for signals of hope we shall discover that every gift and ability in the church is needed, but that all must operate in mutual acceptance, not mutual rejection. A process of cross-fertilization is required, not of instant reaction. Wherever genuine Christian signals of hope are set up, all Christians should rejoice. We will not put the world right in a day but the size of the task did not deter Carey or Hudson Taylor, Mother Teresa or Martin Luther King. It is the planting of the signal within my setting which matters; and the multiplication of single signals will increase the hope of the world, uplifting Christ and honouring the Lord. We may not contain within ourselves the total solution to the problem of integration in our land, but are there not signals of hope we could set up? Our church may not be able to provide employment for the masses who are likely to be unemployed, but are we not able to do something which gives hope to some who are involved in that situation? We may not be able to reach every lonely and needy person in our land, but are our churches not capable of doing more to bring hope at least to some of them? We may not be able effectively to evangelize the whole land, but is it not possible for us to programme our church life so that many more of our resources are used in the task of evangelism, rather than being spent on ourselves? We may not be able to provide all the answers that our modern world asks of life, but is it not possible to see in Jesus Christ the clue to meaning so that we ourselves live lives of hope, and in turn point others to him? It is in the setting up of signals of hope which point towards the nature of our God that we shall be most truly faithful as his people. O Israel, hope in the Lord.

# CHAPTER TWO

# Freedom

*Sermon at the Methodist Conference Service,*
*Eastbrook Hall, Bradford*
*25 June 1978*

TWENTY-FIVE years ago I received my call-up papers for National Service in the Royal Air Force. I duly reported to RAF Cardington, was allocated to a section, received my uniform and equipment, said farewell to my civilian clothing, ate my first meal of cold fish off a sticky mess table, and had my hair (which had been cut a few days before) cut yet again. I was a new recruit, an 'erk', and my brand new uniform constantly provoked the cry 'Get some in' ('some' being months of service), from hoary senior aircraftsmen of nineteen and twenty years of age.

But that was not my major problem. My main concern was how I, as a Christian, was going to maintain my witness. Needless to say, I had received plenty of advice, most of it boiling down to 'start off as you mean to continue'. On the first night I knelt to say my prayers. No boots were thrown, no remarks made. I noticed two other chaps doing the same. I gladly noted them as comrades in a cause.

Then came the invitation to the Station Chapel for a welcome bunfight and a meeting with the Padre. Few in my billet showed any enthusiasm. I tried to encourage them. I ventured a little testimony. Then came the sixty-four thousand dollar question from a chap at the other end of the room, 'What have you got that we haven't, then?' which brought the remark from the already established section comedian, 'A big head!' End of testimony for that evening.

I had learned once more a basic lesson about Christian witness. People need first to see the evidence in our lives before they are ready to listen to the evidence of our lips.

Paul is making this point in Ephesians 4, the controlling lesson for this service. Our text is from verses 22 and 24 of that chapter. 'Put off your old nature . . . put on your new nature' (R.S.V.). If you concentrate on the *verbs* 'put off' and 'put on' you get a picture like that of Cinderella, abandoning the servant girl's rags in order to dress like a princess for the ball. Put off the rags. Put on the finery. But if you turn to the *noun*, 'nature', you are talking about something much deeper. The word literally means 'man'. What Paul tells his readers to put on is the 'new man'. It is nothing as peripheral as dress or appearance. A vital change of *condition* is involved. When a person has been seriously ill and recovers we say, 'he is a new man'. Or if someone has been doing badly and then begins to succeed we say it has made a 'new man' of him. We also use the expression of a person whose moral life has changed for the better. He's a new man.

This is the reply which Paul advocates to the question I faced in the barrack room twenty-five years ago. 'What have you got that we haven't, then?' 'I am a new man, or a new woman, in Christ'. Of course one wouldn't put it that way, but no less an answer will do, however tremblingly and uncertainly we give it. To be a Christian is in some sense to be 'made new'. It is not simply a matter of having a new life-style. It has to do with being a new person.

## 1. A Backward Look

Paul begins by explaining what the Christian is *not*. We cannot in fact, be *only* positive in life. Every positive involves a negative. To be 'free for' I must be 'free from'. In days when tolerance is so highly rated we do well to recall that truth and error, right and wrong, positive and negative are vital considerations for the Christian.

So Paul selects some signposts along the route which Christians should *not* be following (verses 17–19). *'Futility of their minds'* involves a thought pattern often connected with idolatry. It was used by Jews in their criticism of Gentiles. The point is simply that if you worship something which is not God then you make it an idol, and idolatry is futile. But there is also a sense of deliberation—a choosing to worship what is not God—a *commitment* to idolatry. We may feel we are familiar with the problem today living in a culture with so many idols. It was Archbishop William Temple who observed that a mental image is every bit as dangerous as a metal one.

*'Darkened in their understanding'* (verse 18), ties in with Romans 1:21. Since they do not worship the true God, the source of moral and intellectual light, they are progressively in darkness, less and less able to understand. Having turned the wrong way down the tunnel they are not likely to find it getting any lighter.

They are thus *'alienated from the life of God'* (verse 18), neither recognizing nor enjoying it, because of *'their ignorance'* (verse 18) which is an endemic disease among them. As those who commit themselves to oppression and cruelty become less and less aware of the anguish and pain of the oppressed, so those people determined not to serve God become less and less aware of his presence in their lives.

So they *'have become callous'* (verse 19). The word means 'petrified' and is used of stone harder than marble. It also has uses in the medical world, describing the callus formed where a bone has been broken and re-set, a callus which is harder than the bone itself. It can also mean the loss of all ability to feel. In the spiritual realm Caird describes it with the words 'every surrender to temptation encrusts the heart (that is, the will) and narrows the range of its future choice'.

Thus they *'have given themselves up to licentiousness'*, an impudent boastful practice of wickedness, *'greedy to practise every kind of uncleanness'* (verse 19), especially desiring passionately to have what does not belong to them, at cost to others.

This all adds up to a fearful picture of the pathway leading away from God, truth and light. Its most frightening quality is its directional nature. There is a steady and progressive movement downward, little things leading to large ones, small indulgence leading to great indulgence, cherished passions expanding to dominate intellect and will. It is a reminder that most evil begins in a small way, but does not remain small.

## 2. Changing Direction

We may well wonder what chance there is for Paul's readers (or for us for that matter) to go in any other direction when so many on all sides seem willingly committed to a downward spiral of the kind he has described. Yet Paul is sure that his readers not only *can* go in another direction but he knows that they *are already doing so*. He writes to encourage them to keep on travelling.

How did they come to a new experience? Verse 20—they 'learned Christ', that is they 'heard about him and were taught in him, as the truth is in Jesus' (verse 21). There was a body of teaching about Jesus the Christ, which they heard, into which they entered by experience, and which put their feet on to a new road through life. We live in days when experience is rated very highly—and rightly so. The New Testament does not view experience as self-authenticating, however. Beneath and behind valid Christian experience there must be true Christian teaching.

It is significant that Paul separates 'Christ' and 'Jesus' as he does in these verses, since it is not typical of him. However deliberate it is, it serves as a reminder of the link between the Christ they and we experience by faith, and the Jesus who lived in history and could be recognized by sight. To quote Caird again, 'The whole truth about the unseen Christ in whom they are to have their new being is embodied in the historical life, death and resurrection of the man Jesus'. The two are inextricably linked. We enter into the meaning of the earthly ministry of Jesus as we experience the risen Christ. But we know how to recognize the risen Christ by our knowledge of the earthly ministry of Jesus.

But how does knowledge of the historical Jesus and experience of the risen Christ put us on a new path? Here a number of ways of thinking about the Christian life merge into one.

There is the picture of Adam as typifying disobedient rebellious man, and of Christ as typifying obedient and loyal man, each being the first and head of his kind. Since 'Adam' means 'man', the parallel in this verse between the 'old man' and the 'new man' seems fairly obvious—the old man in Adam and the new man in Christ. Our beginning on the new path comes with our decisive break from the natural, human tradition of selfish refusal of God's relationship with us, and the acceptance of a place in his family through Christ. Repentance which literally means 'a change of mind', and 'conversion' (turning round) fit well into this picture.

But how does this actually work out? What process is involved which gives any meaning to this decisive act of turning from Adam's way to Christ's, from old man to new man? Here passages like Colossians 2:10 to 3:17, and Romans 6:1–19 help. Under the picture of baptism, *the believer is seen as being incorporated into the death and resurrection of Jesus Christ.* Passing under the water and surfacing again provided a forceful picture of that incorporation. The New Testament does not simply encourage us *to believe in* Christ's death and resurrection; it commands us to *be buried* with him and *rise* with him. This decisive experience of incorporation is the content of the transaction by which we put our feet on to the new road, as new creatures in Christ.

Put as simply as possible it means that I count myself dead to whatever Jesus Christ died to. He died to sin's power, to rebellion against God, to selfishness. In Christ God counts me—and I count myself—dead to these things also. In his resurrection Jesus Christ rose to declare the power of love, the defeat of sin, the rule of God, the way of forgiveness. In Christ God counts me—and I count myself—in on these things. The direction and perspective of the new person in Christ is provided by all that Christ died and rose for. I put off the old man and put on the new man by incorporation into the death and resurrection of Christ. This is the foundation principle of the Christian life. The risen Christ daily provides the power of his death and resurrection as we by faith walk with and in him.

Of course the Ephesian readers have already begun on this road. Hence the past tense in '*did* not so learn', '*have* heard', '*were* taught'. Their decisive commitment to the new way is in the past. By faith they entered into the new man. Paul now tells them to become what they are: to work out in *fact* what is true of them in *principle*. In *position* they are new men. They are now to show that as their *condition* too. Many soccer players went to Argentina as 'world-class' players. Not all demonstrated themselves to be so.

Christians cannot, and need not try to, achieve this alone however. Alongside the decisive 'put off—put on', there is the continuous *renewing of the mind* (verse 23). When we place ourselves, by faith, into Christ, the power of renewal is given to us. We are not only counted as living by the death and resurrection principle: we are given power to do so. And it is a renewal of our *minds;* a growing in true understanding and right attitudes.

A famous illustration was used at the Keswick Convention many years ago. It told of the man who joined the Navy to see the world, but mostly saw the various decks and floors which a tyrannous bosun forced him to wash day after day. One day, however, he was given his discharge papers as they approached land. The bosun, seeing him packing his kit, ordered him once again to do the servile job he had been forced to repeat week after week. Now, however, he simply refused. At the docks he walked through the various check points free. The discharge papers said he was free, and they had his name on them. So he lived and behaved as a free man. Our being in Christ is the discharge from the way of the old man. We are free to walk as new persons in Christ. Whether it is struggling for justice in society, or speaking a word of personal testimony to Christ, the new person receives power for the task.

### 3. The New Way

Paul says the new nature is 'created after the likeness of God in true righteousness and holiness' (verse 24). Nothing less than the renewal of the image of God within us is the aim! Righteousness and holiness bring a combination of uprightness, justice and devotion. The passion to establish justice in the earth should go hand in hand with commitment to worship. Moral uprightness and private devotion are meant to be of a piece with one another. Whenever the ghastly catalogue of evil, outlined at the beginning of the section, has done its work, the Christian will wish to be effectively in opposition—at personal, family, society, national and international level. Word and deed will both be needed, and so will every christian. For not only is each of us a new person in Christ; we are all corporately part of the one new man whom he is creating.

Whatever else John Wesley's doctrine of Christian Perfection was about, it certainly involved a search for the total re-creation of the image of God in the life of the believer. We act with great integrity as Methodists *and* New Testament Christians as we commit ourselves yet again to be new persons in Christ.

# CHAPTER THREE

# Unity

*Sermon at the Ecumenical Service for
the Methodist Conference,
Bradford Cathedral
25 June 1978*

No ONE imagines the task of achieving christian unity is an easy one. Whether we think of creating something which is not yet present, or of demonstrating openly an invisible unity which has belonged to the church by God's gift from the beginning, the way is a complex and at times painful one. Yet we are here, and that indicates a certain willingness, and perhaps even a commitment to the task.

Our text, Mark 10:45, is not, I think, a usual 'unity' text. It may be that we do the cause of unity little good by searching the Bible for unity texts on such occasions. It could be argued that if christian unity really is dependent upon the content of the gospel itself, and not just a useful addendum to it, then wherever we find gospel material in the Bible we will find an encouragement to unity.

Mark writes, as from the mouth of Jesus, 'For the Son of Man also came not to be served but to serve, and to give his life as a ransom for many' (Mark 10:45 R.S.V.). Dr Vincent Taylor, to whose commentary on Mark many of us are greatly indebted, describes this verse as one of the most important statements in the Gospels. It sees Jesus speaking of himself as Son of Man and foretelling the significance of his death. He uses the metaphor of ransom—a price paid to achieve deliverance. Its uses in the Greek version of the Old Testament and in Classical Greek include the price paid to free the first born from being sacrificed, the purchase of freedom for a relative who was a slave, and the redeeming of a captive. Jesus sees his coming death as the costly act which will set 'the many' free (presumably from divine condemnation of sinners, though that is not stated here). As such this text has been a foundation passage for a particular interpretation of the Atonement for many centuries.

My purpose is not to explore that doctrine, however, but rather to look at Jesus' way of using it in the context of Mark 10;45.

1. *He sees his attitudes and actions as the pattern for the attitudes and actions of his disciples.* The context of this saying in Mark's account is the disagreement among disciples about who should sit on Jesus' right and his left in glory. James and John have asked for the privilege and the other disciples express their displeasure about such a request. Jesus tells them that instead of trying to gain ascendency over one another in that way, they should learn the art of mutual service. The reason for this is that 'the Son of Man also came not to be served but to serve and to give his life as a ransom for many'. Their attitude and action is to be patterned upon his.

Where does such a principle lead us in the matter of unity? One direction will be to ask whether our attitudes and actions towards one another are patterned upon the divine example given to us. The basic theological foundation of christian unity is the doctrine of the Trinity. The inter-relation of Father, Son and Spirit, the mutual honour, love and harmony

*34*

between them, and the varied roles accepted within that relationship, are surely ground for much greater attention than we have so far given them in our unity approaches. Many of our reasons make good common sense—buildings, manpower, resources, effective organization and outreach. But the root reason why the church should show itself one is that God is one. May we not go a little further and ask whether the way in which God is 'three-in-one', with the attitudes and actions involved, may be a pattern for us?

2. *This teaching also demonstrates the essential difference between Jesus and his disciples.* Their attitudes and actions must be patterned upon his, but they cannot achieve what he alone can do. They cannot 'give their lives as ransoms for the many'. Indeed, this way of putting it, with what seem to be echoes of Isaiah 53 and the Suffering Servant, emphasizes the difference between him and them. The one and the many may well mean 'one and the rest'. In Jesus' use of such language there is a clear distinction between himself, Son of man, as 'the one', and everyone else as 'the rest' who can benefit from the ransom he offers.

'The rest' includes the disciples. It also includes us. Here is a second clue to our unity thinking. However diverse we are in outlook and practice we are one in our need of redemption. We have different ways of describing that redemption, and different ways of representing it in our worship. But at the foot of the Cross of Christ we all look remarkably alike. Maybe we would forward the cause of genuinely christian unity if we spent more time telling and listening to one another's stories of redemption, of how God is saving us. It might take longer, but it could involve us all. And it is the stuff of Christianity.

3. *Jesus is talking about their attitude to one another.* The attitude of service which will issue in action is at this point limited to the internal relationships of the group of disciples.

Of course, since they were the only ones present it is not too surprising that he begins there. It is worth noticing, however, that the New Testament as a whole has an emphasis upon christians caring for one another which is difficult to avoid. Indeed, in these days when we constantly encourage one another to care more and more for those outside the church, it is rather embarrassing to admit that our foundation documents in the Scriptures are almost wholly taken up with caring for fellow christians.

Of course good reasons can be advanced to explain this, including the poverty of many early christians. But there does appear to be a christian principle operating here. For New Testament christians it does seem true that 'charity begins at home'. However selfish that might look to us, we do well to ponder it from a slightly different perspective. There are many ways in which New Testament writers look at the church. One is to regard the church as God's pattern for mankind. The community of believers is God's way of incarnating the principles on which life can be lived in harmony, fulfilment and truth. This may be one of the reasons why our Lord is recorded as declaring in John 17 that one purpose of the unity of his followers is that the world might believe. God looks to the church to demonstrate the credibility of fully human life lived in harmony with him and with each other.

In this sense, the call to mutual service *does* begin at home. We must sadly confess that it is often easier to spend our time serving people with no christian commitment (preferably overseas) than to serve fellow christians of a different persuasion from ours.

Could it be that our failure to accept the role of Servant to one another, across our denominations, fails God at a very deep level by denying the world a living pattern of true humanity under God? And could it be that it also undermines much of our service in the world because it does not grow out of our care for one another within the Body of Christ, but is an alternative to it? The world may accept our offers of service: it is not easily deceived about our failure to serve one another.

If this all sounds very costly—costly to cherished ideals and threatening to current practice—let us remember that its setting is the teaching of our Lord and Master who, as Son of Man, 'came not to be served but to serve, and to give his life as a ransom for many'.

CHAPTER FOUR

# Ministry

*Address to Ordinands being received into Full Connexion*
*27 June 1978*

ONE of the less obvious privileges of being a minister is—at
times like Conference and Synod in the ministerial
session—to sit in a room full of ministers. It is in some senses a
strange sight. I have often wondered what would happen if
one were to divest such a gathering of all signs of clerical
apparel, and were then to invite strangers to identify the
common occupation of the group.

Would they see through our disguise as quickly as one does
that of plainclothes policemen, mormon missionaries and
all-in wrestlers at a party? Or would they think of us as civil
servants, school-teachers or a group of trade-unionists on
their annual outing? We certainly do come in a variety of
shapes, sizes, ages and now sexes, though there is mercifully
not a great variety available in the latter category.

If diversity is a hallmark of our ministry then I have to say
that you will be a typical group of ministers! And that underlines two of the gains which the Methodist Church makes
today.

The first is the variety of gifts and graces you bring with you into the work. At your candidature we asked ourselves whether you had the necessary gifts and graces for ordained ministry. We did not expect any of you to have all the necessary gifts and graces in full and equal measure. You probably thought us wrong in that judgment! Maybe you are less sure now!

However that may be, one of the strengths of our ministry, and of itinerancy, is the rich variety within the ranks of our ordained ministers. Our lay brothers and sisters have long ago come to terms with this fact. They do not expect us all to be equally and totally capable in the three areas of greatest expectation of us—pastor, preacher, administrator. Rather they operate a 'swings and roundabouts' attitude towards us. What one lacks the other will provide. And they have a marvellous capacity for awarding marks in each area to our predecessors, and for telling us the score without malice to those who preceeded us or prejudice towards us! May I express the hope that by your life and ministry you may extend the range of their expectations of us beyond that simply of pastor, preacher and administrator? Maybe your presence will enable them to look to ministers to be people of prayer, theologians, facilitators, evangelists, pioneers.

The other great gain the Connexion makes today comes from the variety of your own autobiographies. Many of you would not—in plain clothes—be easily distinguishable from other professions precisely because you have served in those professions. You bring that heritage and expertise with you and you will need it. It both binds you to your lay brothers and sisters as part of the one Body of Christ, and it will still contribute towards making you whole persons. Nor do we forget that some of you, in leaving your professions, are making considerable sacrifices in your income and life-style.

We wish you well as you face the task—by no means an easy one—of relating your autobiography to that of the local churches in which you will serve. The fusion and inter-relationship of all that you are with all that they are can be material for constant strife; but it can also be the basis of proper growth and true discipleshp for all involved. I hope you will find it the latter.

I wish also to remind you—hardly in a fatherly way since it is only sixteen years since I stood where you stand!—that you also gain something today. The Conference standing to receive you into Full Connexion, together with the Ordination which follows, is a symbol that the attitude of Methodism towards you is one of deep trust. You may feel it has taken us a long time to make up our minds! Even if this is so it is because of the seriousness with which we view this moment, and because of the extent of the implications of what we do. Today we accept responsibility for you. If at times you feel Methodists to be critical of their ministers, it is partly because of the high regard in which we are held and because of the degree to which our people feel responsible for us. You may already have found such an attitude both moving and sustaining. Put at its crudest you enter today into one of the safest professions in the working world. Put more feelingly you are given a place of secure esteem within a warm and loving family.

I have talked a great deal about variety and diversity. But at one point we are all the same. We are all called by God in Christ, and enabled by his Spirit to play our part in the task of the church in the world. Paul describes that task as presenting every person mature in Christ. For that task you will need all the gifts and graces you can get—and all the love, prayer and support of the Connexion. That we pledge to you today. God bless you.

CHAPTER FIVE

# History

*Opening Address of the World Methodist Historical Society
(British Section) Conference
25 July 1978*

PEOPLE engaged in historical research—sometimes by choice
but often by the neglect of others—work away from the
limelight. There are exceptions of course, such as a journalis-
tic use (and misuse) of some piece of work, as in the recent
case of Richard Heitzenraters research in John Wesley's
diary. On that occasion parts of the religious press discovered
as new material what many of us have been debating for
years! Apart from such aberrations, however, your work is
often carried out because of your own interest and commitment, which is proper, rather than because of huge popular
support. I hope my presence here today as President of the
Methodist Conference will be a sign that your labours, however enjoyable for you, are also much appreciated by many
others.

I am greatly pleased by your choice of theme. 'Minorities'
and 'Majorities' are much in the news today. At our recent
Conference in Bradford the issue was present in a whole
variety of debates—South Africa and Rhodesia, Ireland, the

closed shop, women on committees. I was even more conscious of this when, at my invitation, leaders of other faiths
met me in Bradford during one evening of Conference. There
is a timely relevance about your chosen theme. I hope I know
too much about historical study as a discipline to speak glibly
about 'the lessons we can learn for today from a study of the
past'. I hope I also know enough, however, to speak with
integrity about the value of historical study in relation to the
problems of the present. Maybe I can best express that value
in terms of perspective.

We live in an age of 'instant' problems and 'instant' solutions. Mercifully for you I have no time to develop that theme
in order to defend it. Suffice it to say that national or international events and incidents are covered on television in about
ten minutes, while the acknowledged experts are expected to
provide their solutions in 90 to 120 seconds on the same
medium. If they cannot describe immediate causes and supply
instant solutions they are likely to be discarded. One hopes
that historical study stands as one buttress against the on-
slaught on truth which is mounted in our modern cultural
setting.

One element in that defence is the concern about evidence
on its many levels. It was, I think, the White House aide
Moynaghan who, on leaving that particular employment,
charged his successors to do their job thoroughly. He quoted
Burkhardt in his prophecy that the late twentieth century
would be the age of the great 'simplificators' whereas what
was needed was a generation of 'complexifiers'. Maybe the
historian's greatest contribution on most occasions is to fulfil
the role of 'complexifier', because he rarely finds matters as
simple and straightforward as others appear to do.

I find, for example, that assertions made and written in
church union negotiations—whether about the benefits of
episcopacy from the Catholic tradition or the honoured place
of lay ministry from the Free Churches—leave me wondering
whether any church historians are present on such commit-

tees, and if so whether their minds are on other things! I have a similar difficulty over many of the solutions offered to current political, social and cultural problems, where historical evidence seems little sought or heeded. I find it also in modern biblical scholarship and wish that more of the devotees of that discipline had begun with degrees in history.

Perhaps most relevantly to this setting, I find the need for more complexification in the study of Methodist history. There have been too few studies like that of Bishop Ted Wickham on Sheffield, and more recently Robert Moore's *Pitmen, Preachers and Politics*. The well-established hypotheses about our origins and development are in danger of becoming more and more firmly established as unassailable interpretations unless they are tested by the complexification of local, specific case studies. Is there room, I wonder, for a fuller, up-dated version of Wesley Swift's booklet on how to carry out historical research? After all, our people, ordained and lay, are very well scattered. Is there a need to be met here so that more of them can be inspired, enabled and guided in doing limited pieces of work which when put together might amount to a sizeable contribution to the task? I am especially concerned about the unwritten recollections retained in the memories of many ageing Methodists, needing to be recorded and followed up. The kind of work you are doing at this Conference could provide the inspiration for which I am asking.

I am one of those who believe that in an ecumenical age there is more need, not less, for clear awareness of the origins, insights, failures and successes of each component part of what is called the 'coming' great Church. I am deeply grateful to you for all that you are doing, and I wish you a most stimulating and invigorating Conference, which I am very happy to declare open.

# II

# THEOLOGY

CHAPTER SIX

# Wholeness in Theology

I BEGIN this chapter with some anxieties about the life of the Church today.

I am concerned about what appears to me to be a fundamental dis-ease in believing, a dis-ease which shows itself locally and generally. At local level it is marked by a lack of a system of believing. I do not mean that our people do not believe enough. They believe a great deal. But so often the things believed do not seem to be organically related. As a friend of mine put it many years ago, 'It is more like a bag of marbles than a bunch of grapes'! The various items of faith do not appear to be related to one another in a recognizable way. They rattle about in the bag, rather than having the growth relationship of grapes in a bunch. When the preacher speaks of 'the faith', therefore, most congregations take him to be referring to an attitude of believing, rather than to the content of what is believed.

Now some may welcome this situation. They may feel it marks a liberation from adherence to tidy doctrinal formulation, learned and repeated without understanding. But even if that is so, the price is a high one to pay. It is very difficult, for example, to build a consistent Christian life-style on the 'bag of marbles' way of believing. It also inhibits a confident and consistent witness, since the Christian has no confidence about answering the questions or enquiries of others. What is more, it becomes very difficult to face any new idea openly, for there is little awareness of how such an idea could relate to anything else. I find this a sign of dis-ease locally.

It is much more serious on a wider scale however. Here it is expressed not so much in terms of incoherence as of division. The Christian Church at large still appears to be divided into two groups. One finds its focal point theologically in Creation—Incarnation—Sacrament. It is largely world-affirming, takes a positive view of culture and has a strong sense of symbolism. The other has its centre of concentration in Redemption—Atonement—Word. Its concern is to save the lost world. It is more conscious of judging contemporary culture. It has high regard for proclamation of the gospel. 'Catholic' and 'Protestant' are now rather tired terms for describing these positions, but they indicate their historical background at least. (Those on each side of the line will rightly feel that the description above is most inadequate. I acknowledge it, but am simply trying to indicate significant directions of thought movement in each case.)

The concern one feels about this difference in theology does not spring from sadness about the division it causes and represents. We are never short of something to divide over! But concern is more justified by the fact that neither position can be properly held or defended without the other. A strong doctrine of atonement and redemption must show why the death and resurrection of Jesus Christ are so significant for human destiny. This can only be done adequately via a strong doctrine of creation and incarnation. Equally those who emphasize creation and incarnation need to bridge the gap between the realities around them and the ideals of their vision in theology. For this they need to affirm redemption and atonement. Without both we are left with an inadequate theology—on either side of the line. We will not find a wholesome theology on either side, for a proper doctrine of God, Christ, Spirit, World, Men, Salvation requires both in harmony.

A second anxiety stems from another division between Christians, between the 'doers' of the gospel and the 'proclaimers' of the gospel. On the one side are those whose basic passion is to be involved in the political and social structures of society. They are striving for a just world. They see how structures inhibit or destroy humanity. In theological terms they wish to establish God's kingdom. On the other side are those whose prime concern is to fulfil their evangelistic calling in the world. They proclaim the gospel to a lost world, they see that the world can be changed only by the change of heart of individuals. They build up and extend the church as the company of heaven. (As before, none will relish either description as adequate. I seek to give the feel of an 'atmosphere' in each case.)

In this situation international documents from Lausanne (Evangelical Congress), Nairobi (World Council of Churches) and Rome (Pope Paul VI), are a great encouragement. Each affirms, though with different points of emphasis, the need for *both* social and political involvement *and* evangelism in the mission of the church in the world. But this could easily become a most dangerous stopping place. We need much more than simply having each side affirming the other, welcome though that is. We need each side listening to the other to discover what is involved for us all in this new convergence. If the socially and politically active seriously affirm the task of evangelism as a proper activity of Christians, one wants to know how they seek conversions and how many they have had. If the evangelist is in earnest about the importance of social and political structures one wishes to learn how this influences his campaigns, his proclamation and his advice to and care of converts. We have a long way to go yet along this particular line of convergence.

A third cause of concern is the Church's failure in apologetic. By this I mean our failure to provide an adequate account of our faith, beginning where people are. Our attempts at communicating the Christian message seem so often to require one particular kind of language and thought-pattern (even one particular class or cultural setting) for any kind of effectiveness. We seem so often to be attempting communication by shouting across a no-man's-land in language and thought-patterns which make it an exercise like shouting advice on room decoration to a colour-blind audience. We feel better for having shouted the message, but the effect is and can only be minimal. We need to discover some way of standing where people are, speaking a language they understand, employing thought forms they can follow and thus enabling them to discover the relevance of our message for life as they now know it. Has any Christian group in our culture learned how to do this effectively?

There is at least one way forward in face of the concerns outlined above. It is to find a more wholesome theology—wholesome in the sense of whole and healthy—than the Christian Church evidences at present. I believe that such a theology is possible if we can achieve the marriage of a new kind of natural theology to a new kind of revealed theology.

Natural theology depends upon a basically inductive process of thinking. That is, it observes life around it, establishes conclusions on a basis of what it observes around it, and then seeks to apply these conclusions in a general and often metaphysical way. A single illustration would be that of the growing child whose mother keeps pointing out various wooden objects and calling them 'chair'. They may not all have exactly the same shape, but there is enough in common for him to discern, on a basis of observation of these objects, what are the essential characteristics of 'chair-ness'.

In this way Christians over the centuries have looked at life around them, observed certain aspects of it, and reached conclusions about God on a basis of their observations. All who have studied theology are likely to have written an essay on the so-called 'proofs' of God's existence. Having summarized the various 'proofs'—cosmological, ontological, teleological, and so on—most will have reached the rather lame conclusion that although the 'proofs' make God more likely than less likely, they can hardly be said to prove him. (The argument, for example, that the presence of design in the universe points to the existence of a designer is impressive rather than conclusive.) A friend of mine put his finger on the weakness of such proofs by saying, 'If an apple pie is put in front of me, it suggests the existence of a cook. But if I were to lift the crust and find the cook standing there I would, to put it mildly, be surprised!'

My own dissatisfaction with the proofs of God was not, however, based on their inadequacy at proving his existence. I do not think I ever expected them to do so. They disappointed me because they were so academic. They were the preserve of the intellectuals, an esoteric band for whom such arguments were both meaningful and interesting. Anyone who has attempted to throw them to a congregation in a sermon will know that they return in one bounce, largely untouched. The proofs thus exclude the majority of the population from an area of theology where all are supposed to be included, since everyday life and experience is the very stuff of natural theology.

I felt I saw the possibility of a new form of natural theology, however, when I read Peter Berger's book *A Rumour of Angels* (Penguin, 1969). Berger writes as a sociologist, testing the hypothesis that modern man has neither the sense of nor the need for the transcendent. As a sociologist he concludes that, on the contrary, large numbers of the species modern man have both a sense of and a need for the transcendent. His evidence is based upon what he calls 'signals of transcendence'. (This approach has relationship to what the late Ian Ramsey called 'disclosure situations' [*Religious Language*, SCM, 1957] and what David Deeks calls 'indicator experiences'[1]).

[1] David G. Deeks, *Doing Theology* (Methodist Church Local Preachers' Department, 1972), Chapter 2.

Briefly, the argument is that certain events, attitudes and actions in everyday life are not capable of a wholly satisfactory explanation in purely natural terms. They require, if they are to be adequately accounted for, some reference to that which transcends our natural understanding of existence. A mother's 'There, there, dear, it will be all right' to a crying child, is seen as an affirmation of the rightness and possibility of order, even though we live in a world of enveloping chaos in human affairs. What is the empirical evidence that 'It will be all right'? Would it not be more in keeping with the facts to say 'It will get worse', or at least 'This is how it always is'? Yet we go on believing in and working for order. It is a signal of transcendence.

Berger also argues from our capacity for play, and our sense of humour, particularly in dangerous and threatening situations. We might well ask ourselves how people can spend any time at leisure in our culture with such distintegration taking place, and such economic problems facing us. And why do war situations produce so much humour? Berger sees in these phenomena our capacity to recognize that even very serious demands upon us are not ultimate. We are capable of leisure even when economic disaster faces us. We can enjoy a joke even in the face of death. (Perhaps we should not say 'even in' but 'particularly in'.) As we do so we are signalling our refusal to accept either economic failure or death as ultimate disasters. Humour and play 'cut them down to size'. But in relation to what? (or whom?) They are signals of transcendence.

We may not particularly like Berger's examples. But he has opened up again the question of whether we are satisfied with wholly naturalistic interpretations of ordinary events of daily life. Maybe it is time for Christians to begin to ask awkward questions of others, instead of always being the ones to provide answers to other people's criticisms. Do we really believe that what takes place at a birth is wholly explicable in a text book on conception and delivery? Or does a psychological and physiological description of love, courtship and marriage accurately and adequately communicate what takes place as two people discover they are in love? And what are we to say of the dying man who tells a visiting friend of the dark night when he felt the power of evil around him and was sustained and delivered as he repeated constantly the words of John Wesley, 'The best of all is, God is with us'. May we not extend the question to a beautiful sunset, a lovely piece of music, a soulful poem, a 'timeless' experience? Are not all these 'signals of transcendence', if only we had eyes to see?

This is surely at least one of the points of Jesus' teaching method. The parable is a most unpromising mode of communication, dealing as it does in very ordinary elements of everyday life. Or could that be its greatest significance? Isn't one purpose of the parable to demonstrate that it is precisely the ordinary, everyday details of life which can become the windows of heaven for those who can perceive their rich texture? We have recently replaced our black and white television set with colour. The difference is striking! One becomes aware of the richness of scenery, crowds, clothing, furniture and even equipment once the colour is visible. Aren't the parables of Jesus one way of showing us that we see life largely in the black and white of material and naturalistic descriptions, but miss the rich colour of the spiritual and transcendent? No doubt they all saw a sower at work, but only Jesus perceived the presence of the kingdom. Is this why he often said 'He who has ears to hear, let him hear'? Is there a perception needed really to understand what life is about?

If all this is true, could it be that there are some particular experiences and events which operate on the border between 'black and white' and 'colour'? Are these the signals of transcendence to remind us that 'colour' is available for all of life? And shouldn't our worship quicken this perception of 'colour' so that every act of worship makes life a more meaningful experience?

But that is to rush ahead. For the moment one simply

wishes to establish a new form of natural theology, whose boundaries are marked out by 'signals of transcendence', 'disclosure situations', 'indicator experiences' or whatever one wishes to call them. And the great strength of such theology is that it is not the possession of the academic or the intellectual only. It is of the stuff of everyday life, of the ordinary areas where scholars are not always renowned for their awareness. It is the space occupied, not only by all Christians but by all human beings.

This form of natural theology ought not to exist on its own, however. Natural theology needs revealed theology more than revealed theology needs natural theology. But each needs the other. Natural theology provides revealed theology with a rootage in daily life. Revealed theology gives natural theology its authentication. It enables us to determine whether or not a particular form of natural theology is truly Christian. In this sense revealed theology is the lead-horse of the pair.

Revealed theology depends upon a deductive process of thinking. It begins with what is revealed, with what is given. It then proceeds to apply the given insights to life round about. In terms of our mother-child analogy it is to learn what is the essential quality of 'chair-ness' first, and then to discover which objects are properly called 'chairs' in the light of that revelation.

There is a tradition of revealed theology just as its 'proofs' were part of a tradition of natural theology. The bulwark of revealed theology parallel to the proofs is the doctrinal formula. Hammered out over the years in debate—and often strife—doctrinal statements are of great value. They are like the cat's-eyes on the road, you are not always aware of their value till you are in darkness or feel lost. But as starting points of communication they are as inadequate as 'proofs'. They, too, bounce back from the congregation largely untouched. Congregations are at a loss to know how to get into the package to grasp the gift of truth contained within.

I felt I saw the possibility of a new form of revealed theology to match the new version of natural theology when I read J. V. Taylor's *The Go-Between God*. Although much of its approach resembles the Berger method, it nevertheless embodies a strong 'revealed' content. One of its major conclusions is that Jesus Christ perfectly embodies much that is deepest in human life—knowing rather than knowing about, giving oneself rather than simply offering help; setting people free rather than just giving them aid. But the perception that these are some of the deepest factors in human life owes a great deal to God's revelation in Christ. For one reader at least this insight was the clue to the book's major contribution.

The value of such a form of revealed theology is that it does not begin with doctrinal definitions. Rather it approaches christology from the point of view of the significance of Jesus Christ. Definitions are necessary, and one cannot get far without them, but it is with the starting point we are concerned. What does Jesus Christ mean? We may take two ways of working out the answer to this question.

Around Christmas time we all hear read to us the magnificent prologue to John's Gospel: 'In the beginning was the Word, and the Word was with God, and the Word was God. He was in the beginning with God; all things were made through him, and without him was not anything made that was made' (John 1:1–3). This is beautiful religion, and the concept of creation by a living Word is a very powerful one. But the dividing point amongst the religions is met a little lower down the chapter: 'And the Word became flesh and dwelt among us, full of grace and truth; we have beheld his glory, glory as of the only Son from the Father' (John 1:14). Here Christianity stands alone. Nor is this John's idea only. Paul in Colossians 1:16 says something similar ('in him all things were created'). So does the writer to the Hebrews in Hebrews 1:2 ('through whom also he created the world'). Now whatever else this means, at very least it seems to be saying that the original word of creation (the principle about which it took place or the agency through which it happened), is that which the disciples encountered in the life of Jesus Christ. No wonder John continues 'in him was life, and the life was the light of men' (John 1:4). He is affirming that Christ is the clue to all created life.

The implications of this are very far-reaching indeed. It means that the life they witnessed as Jesus Christ—the attitudes and acts, the self-giving and liberating influence, the perceptions of God and of the world, and above all the life-death-resurrection pattern of existence—all these are meant to be at the centre of created life. They are the heartbeat of creation. Unless life finds its source here then it is no better than a human body which tries to neglect its heart. Debates about incarnation as a model for understanding Jesus Christ will miss the point unless they can grapple with the problem at this level.

The relevance of this way of picturing Christ is not hard to find. Since he is the way not only to salvation of the individual but also to created life itself, then to know him is not only to know one's sins forgiven and to enjoy new birth. It is also to understand for the first time what life is about. From this source we may begin to perceive life's divine colours replacing our human black and white. In Christ all of life takes on a new significance.

But it goes further than that. If Christ is the clue to life's meaning, then all the major problems facing the world—pollution, ecology, starvation, underprivilege and the like—require as base material for their solution the life, death and resurrection of Jesus Christ. That is not the only material needed. A grasp of theology alone does not enable or authorize us to pronounce on all subjects! But it will be base material for understanding how such problems ought to be met. One thinks, for example, of how much the world needs to understand grace as it faces its problems. Yet grace is what Jesus Christ is about. This kind of revealed theology is both desperately needed and in tragically short supply at the moment.

A second way of working at revealed theology in terms of the significance of Jesus Christ concerns his death and resurrection. Of course Christians wish to go beyond a merely political interpretation of his death. ('He died because he was a scandal to Jewish leaders and an embarrassment to Roman officials.') They would be wise to go further and affirm that the death and resurrection of Jesus reveal the depth of God's love for his creation and the indestructability of that love. 'For God so loved the world that he gave his only Son, that whoever believes in him should not perish but have eternal life' (John 3:16). 'But God raised him up, having loosed the pangs of death, because it was not possible for him to be held by it' (Acts 2:24). They also see the link between human sin and Christ's death and resurrection: 'For if we have been united with him in a death like his, we shall certainly be united with him in a resurrection like his. We know that our old self was crucified with him so that the sinful body might be destroyed, and we might no longer be enslaved to sin. For he who has died is freed from sin. But if we have died with Christ, we believe that we shall also live with him. For we know that Christ being raised from the dead will never die again; death no longer has dominion over him. The death he died he died to sin, once for all, but the life he lives he lives to God. So you also must consider yourselves dead to sin and alive to God in Christ Jesus' (Romans 6:5–11). These insights are basic to Christians, contained in our teaching, represented in our sacraments, confirmed in our experience.

Personally I wish to affirm the centrality of that way of understanding the death and resurrection of Jesus Christ. But I must go on to ask whether that is all one can say about these events. And I do not believe that it is.

When Jesus, in John's Gospel, is recorded as preparing his disciples to understand his death, he uses the analogy of a grain of wheat: 'Truly, truly, I say to you, unless a grain of wheat falls into the earth and dies, it remains alone; but if it dies, it bears much fruit' (John 12:24). The setting in that chapter is the declaration of his manifesto. ('The hour has come for the Son of Man to be glorified', John 12:23.) But the way of glorification is by death and new life—like the way of the grain of wheat, put down into the dark earth and hidden from the sight or awareness of men till new life begins to spring up through the soil.

Is Jesus saying here that his death and resurrection are the supreme example of a principle which is constantly at work in nature, and lived through in every cycle of the seasons? In his case it is the supreme and unique example because it is full of divine love in its perfection—as he was. Yet the principle is the same.

This interpretation finds support in the way Jesus then applies the same principle to his followers: 'He who loves his life loses it, and he who hates his life in this world will keep it for eternal life. If any one serves me, he must follow me; and where I am, there shall my servant be also; if any one serves me, the Father will honor him' (John 12:25-6). They too are to enter into the same experience with him, an experience represented in our sacrament of baptism, as the Romans 6 passage, quoted above, suggests.

And isn't this principle capable of still wider application? Couldn't human history be written in these terms? The development of civilization, the rise and decline of empires, the transformation of ideas, the birth, decay and replacement of institutions by others are all examples of the process. So is much of our modern technological advance.

It is surely here that the Christian revealed theology has so much to contribute. The principle of death and resurrection will operate anyway. It appears to be part of the mechanism of history. But its supreme example in the death and resurrection of Christ demonstrates how the process should work. It requires the exercise of *self-giving love* whose concern is the well-being of others, especially the needy. It needs to be expressed in *grace,* love-in-action which does not require the loved one to be lovely, but gives itself for others because it is its nature and because they need what it has to give, even if they do not recognize it. And it must have a foundation in *truth,* in terms of knowledge and morality. In other words it must operate on the basis of the deepest possible understanding of life and all that it involves. And it must have as its aim the highest good for all concerned. It is the absence of these divinely-revealed-in-Christ qualities of love, grace and truth which makes the death and resurrection principle so painful to bear in international, national, local and personal affairs. Without their presence we operate at a much shallower level, where selfishness and legalism so easily take over, where profit becomes more important than people, where the system overwhelms persons and we find ourselves caught up in something too big for us. It is the insights of revealed theology, in the life, death and resurrection of Christ which at this point are most significant. Only then can the 'death-and-resurrection' principle be properly experienced.

I believe that this kind of revealed theology, based on the significance of Jesus Christ, could be effectively linked to the kind of natural theology outlined earlier. They are not operating in two different worlds but in the one world where God has his dwelling with men. They both illuminate the hidden as well as the visible. And they demonstrate Jesus Christ to be both the unique man and the Son of God, embodying in himself immanent and transcendent reality. In him the divine colour is constantly transforming the human black and white, time is infused with eternity, everything secular is touched by the sacred.

What is more, this all relates to life as we all know it. There is a chance here for belief to be coherent because its setting (our everyday life) provides the materials for faith. And every part of life is influenced by this way of believing. The coherence of belief is derived from the totality of life to which it relates. The content of the faith is not something existing over against us. As we put the pieces of the jig-saw together they form the pavement on which we stand, the ground over which we walk.

What is more, the creation/redemption, incarnation/atonement, sacrament/word divisions are no longer tenable. The gap is bridged by Christ. In him we see how what God is relates to what the world is. In him God's presence is every-where detected in life. In him life's potential is everywhere located in God. The creation needs redemption. Incarnation moves inexorably towards atonement. Sacrament requires the explication of the word. Yet redemption needs creation as its arena, atonement needs incarnation as its basis, word needs sacrament as its complement. Wholeness stems from their mutual inter-dependence. 'Doers' and 'proclaimers' can no longer justify their separate existence.

Here is the ground for a genuine apologetic which begins where people are. The di-polarity of natural and revealed theology now operates within the one force-field, namely life as it has been transformed by the ministry of Jesus Christ. The discontinuity between man's search for God and God's find-ing of man becomes a continuity as Jesus Christ bridges the gap. And man's side of the gap is wherever any man, woman or child is standing, sitting, lying, walking or running.

When first sailing to Nigeria I stood on deck one night. The light of the moon shone across the waves, illuminating the water. Neither could do without the other if the scene were to be complete. However far the ship sailed the light appeared to be coming straight to us. One felt one could dive into the water and follow the line of light to the very moon itself. Natural and revealed theology, properly understood and joined, assure us that divine light does reach us where we are, and that we need only cast ourselves in to discover the buoyancy of living by faith.

# CHAPTER SEVEN

# The Content of the Gospel

'Why do we seem to have good news which nobody wants?' My friend was expressing the frustration which Christians often feel. (This may be one reason why the Gospel writers include the parable of the Sower.) In a culture like ours, where so many seem simply to ignore the church and its message, it is hardly surprising if Christians become perplexed by the lack of response to what—to them—is so significant a message.

Of course my friend was exaggerating somewhat. Many do respond to our message, and they are not all teenagers either. Lists of new members in the Methodist Church certainly reveal that young and middle-aged couples, and old people, are joining the Church.

Yet he had put his finger on a tender spot. And it is little comfort to know that the early Christians may have found it a puzzle too. True, the parable of the Sower might be better named the parable of the Soils. Its message is that no matter how good the seed, if it falls into a hostile context it won't produce fruit. However clearly we communicate the message it may be rejected. People are both free to choose and required to do so. We must not force them. They are responsible for their choice.

We need to be sure, however, that the seed we are sowing is the genuine article. Deliberate resistance by the hearers is not the only possible reason for the rejection of our message. It could be that the story we told was not the authentic Christian gospel. Or it may have been a partial rather than a complete account. Of course we all have much to learn about the content and the implications of our message. We do well to be constantly examining ourselves in this respect, and especially those of us whose privilege and task it is to preach or teach.

What is the good news, then? The moment we ask that question we come up against a number of problems. The first has to do with *perception*. How are we going to locate the good news? By what method will we gain the knowledge required to give 'content' to the message?

Every kind of knowledge has an appropriate discipline by which it can be discerned. If we wish to speak German we shall have to use the appropriate methods for achieving linguistic skill. If one wishes to be a doctor then the disciplines of medical science will have to be mastered. If one intends to understand literature then the art of literary criticism will have to be practised. Every bit of knowledge is available via the discipline appropriate to it.

The difficulty with the gospel is that it is composed of at least two kinds of knowledge. It is partly to do with things which happened. Christians believe that God acted in history in a way which was different from anything that had happened before or has happened since. We say that God acted in history through Jesus Christ. This means that some of the knowledge involved in the gospel must be accessible to historical research. It is right and proper for Christians to go on asking what actually happened in the ministry of Jesus, what he said and did, and how much can be known about him.

That is not sufficient of itself however. The Christian Church is not a sacred form of historical society. There is another kind of knowledge of the gospel. That is the knowledge which comes from faith. The writer to the Hebrews says

'By faith we understand . . .' (Hebrews 11:3). There are many Christians who know little or nothing about historical disciplines who nevertheless have a well-grounded experience of Christ. They may not know how to establish the historical veracity of the gospel stories, but they have perceived their significance and live convincingly in the light of that perception. By contrast there are those who by historical method can demonstrate the essential likelihood of certain deeds and words of Jesus and yet are not themselves Christians.

The discipline of establishing historical likelihood and the discipline of faith are needed by the church. Not all Christians can be adept at the first, but all need the second. And those who do not have a capacity for historical discipline are dependent on those who do. They assume an historical authenticity which they know that others can demonstrate. The trouble is that so often these two ways have been viewed as opposites or alternatives, rather than as complementary one to the other. Some recent books have sought to redress the balance.[1] Historical endeavour without scepticism and faith without obscurantism need each other if the good news is to be properly apprehended.

The second problem is about *sensitivity*. In particular it is about recognizing different levels of truth and different ways of expressing truth. Take the statement 'Darling, I love you with all my heart'. There are different ways of expressing truth even in that short and much used sentence. Even allowing for the complexity of human nature, the 'I' and the 'you' are reasonably easily understood. One could build up a comprehensive file on each—birth, parenthood, nationality, education, ability and so on. But what are we to make of 'love'? How does one begin to perceive what that means as between these two people. And what about 'with all my heart'? One can imagine the fun a medical man would have with that! Yet

[1] I. H. Marshall, *I believe in the Historial Jesus,* (Hodder and Stoughton, 1977); C. F. D. Moule, *The Origin of Christology*, (Cambridge University Press, 1977); E. L. Mascall, *Theology and the Gospel of Christ*, (SPCK, 1977); J. N. D. Anderson, *The Mystery of the Incarnation*, (Hodder and Stoughton, 1978).

we talk about 'raining cats and dogs' without our ringing the RSPCA.

If we are to understand the good news, the gospel of Jesus Christ, we shall need a proper sensitivity to different levels of truth and different ways of expressing truth. It is a land full of hills and valleys as well as milk and honey. If we reduce it to a plain we may miss the harvest also.

Our third problem concerns *description*. How are we to categorize the contents of the message so that they are most clearly comprehended? How are we to approach it in such a way that we and others may understand it as clearly as possible?

The traditional way is to describe the events in series. 'First Jesus was born, then he grew up. He taught and healed. Then he was crucified. He rose again and appeared to his disciples. Later he ascended. He will one day return in triumph.' The 'events in series' method has a long tradition in many disciplines. Thus one can describe a piece of Mozart by saying 'First there is a quiet piece. Then he moves into a loud section. After that he lifts you to the heights of ecstasy, then casts you down to the depths of sadness. Finally he gathers all the themes together into one short section which concludes the piece.' It is orderly. It is clear. It corresponds to the developments as they take place.

There is another way to describe Mozart, however. It is not to recount the movement through the music as it is played, but rather to pin-point those characteristics of his music which are essentially Mozart. 'Do you know any composer who so employs the entire key-board?' 'Have you heard any other music which so relates soaring joy and deep pathos?' 'Can you think of anyone else who can gather so many themes together in one short section and make you feel they have always belonged to one another?' The search is now on, not for a description of events in series, but for the basic elements of the entity being described. Where those are present you have authentic Mozart. Where they aren't, you haven't!

66

A similar approach may help to take us much more deeply into the content of the gospel than we have hitherto gone. We are looking for those authentic elements which are the heart of the message. Wherever you cut into a stick of Blackpool rock you find the word Blackpool. Wherever you cut into the gospel there are certain constituent elements to be found.

The first is *event*. There is about the gospel a 'given-ness', a 'happened-ness'. It centres upon what God did in Christ. Scholars continue to debate how much in the Gospels is description of events, and to discuss whether we have the criteria and materials with which to answer the question. But all are agreed that there were events. Things happened in the life of Christ which were the point of radical departure for human history. After those events nothing could ever be the same again because they were A.D. and not B.C.

This means that the foundation of the gospel is something which God did through Jesus Christ centuries ago. In one sense I do not have to think up what to say in next Sunday's sermon. The basic material is given in the story of Jesus Christ. It is written into history, and whatever else you can do with history, you erase it out or cause it to 'unhappen'. You can malign it, criticize it, interpret it or ignore it, but you cannot rub it out. Next time you have a birthday you can only be the age you are. To pretend that you are a different age or a different person would be an act of folly and would lack integrity. Yet your age, sex, heredity, colour, genes were all 'given'. The only thing to do is to respond to that which is given in the most fulfilling way.

Our task as bearers of the good news is not to think up our clever arguments, nor to find ways of commending ourselves or the church. It is not primarily to produce good answers to pressing questions. First and foremost it is to tell the story of Jesus Christ so that hearers can see the implication. If God gave himself to us in Christ, then the logical thing for us to do is to give ourselves to him. It is an enormous strength at the basis of our task. God has acted and we tell the story. Do we tell it enough? While recording some broadcast talks I was stopped by the producer with the words, 'At that point you are working too hard'. I knew why. Having begun on a topic of general interest I had now reached the 'God bit'. In order to get the message over I was screwing up all my energy, concentration and endeavour. The producer went on, 'Your material is good enough in itself. Just tell it'. Maybe we need to remember that when telling the story of Jesus. It will come as news to many of our fellows—and as moving and convincing news to some.

Events alone, however, are not enough. They require *interpretation*. The man who shakes your hand and smiles is judged to be adopting an attitude of benevolence towards you. But the handshake and smile are events with an agreed interpretation. We shake hands and smile in order to communicate benevolence. Events need interpretation if their significance is to be clear.

It is so with the events of the gospel also. And the writers show awareness of this. In Matthew 1:21 for example, we read of the birth of a baby which is about to take place ('she will bear a son'). It is described as an event to take place. There follows immediately, however, information about the name of this child ('You shall call his name Jesus, for he will save his people from their sins'). Later in verse 23, using an Old Testament prophecy, the writer records 'his name shall be called Emmanuel (which means, God with us)'. The birth is regarded as an event, but the giving of the names is about interpretation. They are to tell us *what the event means.*

Again one must note that scholars discuss the relationship between these two, and how clearly we can distinguish them. But however minimal one judges the event element to be, it is still there, and so is the corresponding interpretation.

Have we taken this strand in the gospel seriously enough, I wonder? There may be many in our churches who love the events. They attend services, particularly on the great festivals. They love Christmas and Easter, Whitsuntide and Harvest. They can recount the events which lie beneath the celebration. But has the meaning ever reached them? Have they been gripped by the interpretations? The two are so close together in the New Testament. In Mark 1:14 we are told that 'Jesus came into Galilee preaching'. The significance of that event is in the message he proclaimed: 'The time is fulfilled, and the kingdom of God is at hand; repent, and believe in the gospel' (Mark 1:15). In Mark 10:45 we read that 'the Son of Man came not to be served but to serve and to lay down his life'. This is a statement of the event of his death. But it goes on 'as a ransom for many'. This is the interpretation. Do all who enjoy Christmas realize that it means Jesus—a saviour from sin? Do all who follow through the story of Easter grasp that his death is a ransom for them? Do all who join in the resurrection hymns see that it can mean the presence of the living Christ in their lives by faith? Maybe we jump too quickly in our preaching from the event to the illustration and on to the application, forgetting that interpretation is vital if the event is to have meaning for the hearer. How many Christians understand, for example, that the death and resurrection of Jesus Christ do not simply mean that God's love is available to us, but also that those who trust in Christ are 'counted in' on his death and resurrection? (Buried with him and raised with him as Paul puts it in Romans 6.) Event and interpretation each need the other.

To those we must add *projection*. The New Testament writers faced more questions than simply what to include and how to present it. There was a question initially of readership and ultimately of relevance. In some cases we are told for whom a particular Gospel or letter was written. In others we have to guess. Yet however the particular situation determines the presentation, we are given to understand that the basic message is of much wider application than to those readers. The question is 'How wide?' The tendency to answer 'For Jews only' is clearly revealed in Luke's account of the Council of Jerusalem in Acts 15. With a struggle they decided that Gentiles too were accepted. But was it only for the areas where Jews were? Was it only for the Roman Empire? Was it only for the first century? How broad was the perspective in which they were to view Jesus Christ?

They had to come at that question from another angle too. How were they adequately to account for what he was and what he had done? Categories of healer, teacher, revolutionary did not appear to satisfy them. But how could they go much beyond that without saying what they had never dreamt they would say about any man? How were they to paint a true picture? Which backcloth was sufficiently spacious?

They answered both questions—who he was for and who he was—in a quite startling way. In John 1:1–14; Matthew 7:21–23; Colossians 1:15–16; Hebrews 1:2, there are examples of the answer. On a basis of what they had seen, heard and experienced of Jesus Christ, in the light of God's dealings with the Old Testament people and, we may believe, under the guidance of the Holy Spirit, they interpreted Jesus Christ against the widest back-cloth of all—eternity. In John, Colossians and Hebrews he is seen as the one who was before the world came into being, and as the one through whom it came into being.[2] You look as far back as you can and he is. In Matthew, Colossians and Hebrews the projection is also forward. He is the one in whom all things will be seen to make any sense at all. When all things are wound up, he will still be. The only perspective by which one can properly view him, they seem to be saying, is that of eternity. Anything smaller is too cramping for you to appreciate all there is to know.

We are familiar with this at a purely human level. We could all think of outstanding people—politicians, thinkers, artists, writers, religious leaders—whose gifts, capacities, insights and abilities mark them out as 'world size'. They need the whole world as their context. And we need to see them in that

---

[2] For a fuller examination of this concept and its significance see page 57 ff.

70

setting fully to appreciate their greatness. The New Testament writers are saying that it is so with Jesus Christ; only the setting is not the world here and now, but all worlds for all time. He is eternity-shaped.

This is why you can neither effectively secularize the gospel nor separate it from everyday life. You cannot secularize it because it centres on a person whose being extends beyond realms which the secular is capable of touching or comprehending. You cannot separate it from everyday life because the temporal is included within the eternal. The 'here-and-now' is part of the 'always-everywhere'. Jesus Christ is Lord not only of personal forgiveness and eternal destiny. He is Lord of all being. Does our understanding of the good news include this strand? And how well do we communicate how large Christ is?

One has to face the fact, however, that all of the foregoing could be high-sounding theory. They may, of course, possess a certain relatedness-to-things-as-they-are. But how does one know that they are true in the sense of making any difference? It is here that a fourth strand is discernible. There is *testimony*. John says, 'We have beheld his glory' (John 1:14). In I John 1:1–2 we read, 'That which was from the beginning, which we have heard, which we have seen with our eyes, which we have looked upon and touched with our hands, concerning the word of life—the life was made manifest, and we saw it, and testify to it'. Paul's comment (after listing the people to whom the risen Christ appeared) is, 'last of all, as to one untimely born, he appeared also to me' (I Corinthians 15:8). There is an earthing takes place when events, interpretation and projection are appropriated into an ordinary life by faith. A claim is not true because we experience it, but our experience enables us to enter into its truth. And it helps those who have not yet entered into the Christian faith when they hear how it was and is for others.

After I had lectured at Cliff College in Derbyshire a student asked, 'Where is the place for testimony in a Methodist service?' I replied, 'Liturgically anywhere, but actually nowhere'. My concern is not to defend the formal testimony when someone tells us how he became a Christian. It is a much larger matter than that, though it includes it. I am wishing to safeguard the place in all our preaching and in all our telling of the good news, for that recounting of experience—ours or others—which helps people to see how the great gospel truths have been and can be experienced in our time. For many of our fellows the way into most new experiences and situations is opened up by the evidence of others concerning what they have done and experienced. We should neither despise nor neglect this way—and particularly if our own path into truth is more rational and cerebral. Maybe much of our preaching and personal witness could do with more of the spirit of Peter and John, as recorded in Acts, when faced with a prohibition against preaching: 'We cannot but speak of what we have seen and heard' (Acts 4:20).

Then there is also *application*. It seems to be a basic principle of Christian truth that what you believe must show in what you are. It is also a safeguard against self-delusion and false pietism. John Wesley used to ask his followers about 'the evidences' whenever they claimed deep spiritual experiences. Much of the debate about 'faith' and 'works' misses the quite basic point that both are necessary in a well-balanced Christian life.

We do well to avoid seeking to control the application of Christian truth to other people's lives, however. The story of Legion in Mark 5 is surely a warning here. After his demon-possession has been cured Legion, not unnaturally, seeks to join the disciples in the boat. But Jesus, surely to everyone's surprise, sends Legion home to tell his friends and relatives what has happened to him. The Lord keeps his disciples much longer yet, before trusting them to go off, and then they go 'two-by-two'. But this man, whose life had been so recently and dramatically changed from a terrifying and dangerous instability, is trusted to go alone and represent the faith. How differently we would have settled that issue, helping Legion 'in the boat' till adequately trained and trusted (by which time he might have become largely incapable of communicating his dramatic experience to his own people). *That* there is application of spiritual truth we may be sure. *What* it is for other people we may often have to wait and see—and accept. Do we preachers believe that God will speak through our words so that the truth is applied to people's lives? And do we believe that it can be so applied in ways of which we ourselves are unaware?

Finally there is *invitation*. There is about the story of the good news that which is intended to excite curiosity. 'Why make so much fuss about one baby born so many years ago? Weren't there many babies born that day?' You will have to listen to what happened and what was said to answer that. 'But why such attention to what this particular teacher and healer was doing and saying? Weren't travelling rabbis a common sight?' You will need to ponder the words and consider the significance of the deeds from closer in to know about that. 'If he does and says so much that is good, why are they bent on destroying him, and why doesn't he escape?' You will need to stand very close to him on the road to Jerusalem to hear what he is saying, or kneel with him in the garden at Gethsemane if you really seek answers. 'And what is the point of this hideous death on the cross?' Listen to what he is saying. 'What's all this about him being raised from the dead? That sort of thing doesn't happen, does it?' Get as near as you can and listen to the disciples. 'But how can I be sure it is true?' You can't from the outside. You need to step inside the circle of faith, trusting your life to this Jesus Christ. Only then can you discover the reality.

> 'O make but trial of His love;
> Experience will decide
> How blest they are, and only they,
> Who in His truth confide.'

> (M.H.B. 427)

Or, as John's Gospel puts it somewhat more succinctly, 'Come and see' (John 1:39, 46).

Here are six elements in the gospel story which are quite basic. They are the strands which make up the rope. Any one of them provides a starting point for telling the story, but each needs all the rest for fullness and wholeness.

Maybe if our good news came over like this more people would want it. . . .

CHAPTER EIGHT

# The Theology of the Wesleyan Movement

*Lecture to the World Methodist Council Executive Committee,*
*High Leigh, Hoddesdon*
*31 October 1978*

I BEGIN with some of the problems inherent in the title itself. (I didn't choose it; but I accepted it, so I can't escape responsibility for it!) Which Wesleyan Movement do we mean? The original impetus in England alone? Or that beginning plus its various developments in Great Britain since, through Wesleyan, Primitive, United Methodist and into the Methodist Church today (though with a variety of groups still outside its boundaries, such as the Wesleyan Reform Union, Continuing Primitive Church, and others)? Or do we include the huge addition of the Americas, Africa and Asia? And even could we solve the problems of space and time we would still have to face the problem of a third level. What about the theology of Wesleyan Movements which continue without using the name—as, presumably, is the case in Australia, Belgium, Canada and South India at least?

Next there is the problem—beyond time, space and ecclesiastical circumstance—of the cultural setting and autobiography of any given Wesleyan group. To be small or large, or to be comparatively small or large (and the two are not the same thing—as witness the 'large' Tongan Methodist Church with 10,000 but the 'small' Burmese Church with 13,000), can influence one's theological emphases considerably.

I have decided—in face of this mountain of problems—to operate between two poles. On the one side we shall look at some of the major emphases of John Wesley himself, though not in terms of the so-called four 'alls' of Methodism, namely, that all men need to be saved, that all men may be saved, (though not that all will be saved), that all men may know themselves saved, and that all men may be saved to the uttermost. On the other we shall enquire into the significance of those emphases for today. I am encouraged in this approach by the words of Dr Albert C. Outler in his stimulating work *Theology in the Wesleyan Spirit:* 'He (Wesley) is, I also believe, a very considerable resource in our own time for *our* theological reflections, especially for those who have any serious interest in the ecumenical dialogue and in the cause of Christian Unity' (op. cit., p. 1) If I do not say much about unity and the catholic spirit, it is because I see it as the inevitable backcloth of everything else. Dr Outler goes on to speak of Wesley as 'a creative Christian thinker with a special word for *these* parlous times and for us, as we try to grapple with the new problems created by the current crises in culture . . .' (ibid., p. 2). Since we are part of the 'Wesleyan Movement' by our common allegiance to a Church founded by God through John Wesley, I want to ask whether we also share a common awareness of the implications of Wesley's teaching for today.

I begin with his understanding of prevenient grace. It is a commonplace in Wesleyan scholarship that much of Wesley's doctrine stems from his doctrine of sin. (It is probably true of all of us!)

'Wesley's definition of sin is important. In the judgment of some scholars, the variant reactions to his doctrine turn largely on the view taken of this definition.' This statement by Dr W. E. Sangster asserts the importance of relating Wesley's belief about natural man to the rest of his doctrine. *Lindström* claims that 'The Fall and its consequences are fundamental in his doctrine of justification'; while Sangster sees it as 'one of the most determinative influences on his finished view of perfection'. In examining the nature of this influence the *first requirement* is a clear definition of Wesley's doctrine of the Fall and Original Sin.

His doctrine of the Fall begins with a *picture of man as made in the image of God*—holy, merciful, perfect, living in love—'an incorruptible picture of the God of glory'. This was a threefold image of God; the natural, the political and the moral. To man in this condition God gave a perfect law, legitimately requiring total and continual obedience; and 'superadded' one positive law concerning the fruit of the tree. But although holy and wise, and capable of keeping God's law, man also possessed free will, and was therefore also capable of falling. He preferred his own way, longed to find happiness in the world and in his own work, and so rebelled against his Creator. In other words, *the cause of the Fall was the operation of man's free will over against the loving will of God his Creator.* The *result* was *disastrous.* Thereby he lost God's favour; the moral image of God was destroyed (though the natural and political aspect were only partially affected); man's love for God and knowledge of him disappeared; he suffered spiritual, temporal and eternal death. He had chosen the way of pride and self-will and thus, 'dead in spirit, dead to God, dead in sin, he hastened on to death everlasting'. There can be little doubt that Wesley kept close to the Reformers here, and would have agreed with Hooker's dictum, 'The best things we do have somewhat in them to be pardoned', stating himself that all man's works are 'unholy and sinful themselves, so that every one of them needs a fresh atonement. Only corrupt fruit grows on a corrupt tree.'

*This sin of Adam was imputed to the whole human race.*

Here Lindström appears to be correct in associating Wesley's view with that of Augustine in relation to Paul's doctrine of original sin. Adam is seen as 'the common father and representative of us all'. The fact is asserted, but the manner is never explained, that everyone sinned in Adam; that his disobedience made all men sinners; and that his descendants are therefore void of spiritual life from their very birth. *His definition of original sin varies.* Sometimes it means an inclination towards evil, sometimes a total corruption of man's whole nature. *But the effects are clear.* It gives rise to all sins, it is responsible for corruption, guilt and punishment, and it has both corporate and individual implications. It is demonstrated by the lives of the children of good parents, by observation of the world around, and by personal experience. As J. E. Rattenbury remarks of Charles, 'If he had had doubt about original sin he would have looked into his own heart.'

*Yet no man is damned because of Adam's sin alone.* Original sin and its guilt are distinguished from personal sin and guilt, the latter being the result of deliberate choice of evil despite God's grace offered to keep man pure. Thus, those who choose to live shall live. Those who die spiritually have chosen to do so. Thus Wesley rejects the idea of 'Calvin's irresistible God and passive helpless clay—man'. His Arminian view of election modifies the Reformed doctrine of Original Sin to this extent.

Man's response is a genuine one of repentance and faith. At first, soon after 1738, faith is his major emphasis. But increasingly, and especially by reason of his struggles against antinomian tendencies, he stresses not only repentance but fruits of repentance, though these are never viewed as meritorious. Faith is demanded because corrupt, rebellious man can have salvation no other way except by simple receipt of a gift. Repentance is demanded, because inbred sin is so deep that men may deceive themselves.

*The problem was how man could be in such a parlous state, and make a genuine response.* To veer in one direction lands one into the gloom of Calvinistic predestinarian views: to go the other way brings one to the Pelagian path which casts doubt upon our salvation as stemming wholly from the free grace of God.

The clue by which Wesley perceived another possibility is the doctrine of prevenient grace. As Williams puts it, 'He insisted on the one hand, that man cannot move himself toward God, being entirely dependent on God's enabling grace. But he also insisted that man is responsible before God for his own salvation, being free to accept God or reject him'. (Colin W. Williams, *John Wesley's Theology Today,* p. 40). In Wesley's own words, 'Salvation begins with what is usually termed (and very properly) *preventing grace;* including the first wish to see God, the first dawn of light concerning his will, and the first slight transient conviction of having sinned against him. All these imply some tendency towards life; some degree of salvation; the beginning of a deliverance from a blind unfeeling heart, quite insensible of God and the things of God' (Sermon LXXXV, 'Working out our own salvation', *Works of John Wesley,* vol. VI, p. 509). That this operation of prevenient grace is closely related to conscience is shown in his Sermon CV, 'On Conscience', (*Works,* vol. VII, pp. 186 ff.) The major point all through however, is that by the operation of prevenient grace (a supernatural, not a natural gift of God, *Works,* vol. VII, p. 187) man is enabled to face salvation as an option, but an option which wins him no merit. He is neither inevitably lost, nor inevitably saved. Choice is before him, but only as a gift of grace. To choose the right way brings no merit, because it is the fruit of God's work in us. To choose the wrong way brings no injustice to us, for we have chosen against God's grace.

This insight provides the alternative both to Calvinistic pessimism and to Pelagian optimism. It is a major clue to Wesley's doctrine of Salvation.

My question is whether we take it seriously enough. It is the key to all else. Without this step, nothing else follows. It is as a person feels his way towards the good, or is uneasy in the presence of the evil, and both because he is sensible of God and the things of God, that he approaches the 'porch of religion: which is repentance, preceding faith (the door) and holiness (religion itself) *(Works,* vol. VIII, p. 472, Principles of a Methodist Farther Explained).

If this is such a crucial area, it may be that some of our failures in evangelism stem from our neglect of it. To begin nearest home, is there a tendency for preachers to invite faith in Christ before their hearers are in a position to see why faith in Christ is necessary at all? Are we offering good news which no one seems to want, because they do not yet know why they should want it? Slightly further out is the question whether we *believe* that sin *is* humankind's major problem for which faith in Christ is the solution. In an age in which the church has gone quiet about sin it is often the world which talks about it, though usually in terms of man's sin against man rather than man's sin against God. And still further out we must ask whether we believe in a supernatural operation of God on or in the conscience of human beings leading them towards him. It is an enormous encouragement to sensitive evangelism. It becomes a work of co-operating with the Spirit of God in his work.

So the largest question of all, concerns the area we some-times call pre-evangelism. Wesley expected much of the op-eration of prevenient grace to take place through the word of the preacher (witness his own) and in a setting where the existence of God was commonly assumed. How are we to co-operate with God's work of prevenient grace in cultures where the preacher is not heard by the vast majority and where the existence of God is either unconsidered or flatly denied? The parable of the Sower is not about the skill of the Sower or the high quality of the seed. These are taken for granted. It is about a certain inevitability of growth or decay, given the condition of the ground which receives the seed. Maybe our very belief in prevenient grace ought to cause us to heed the missionary poster which said, 'Don't sow a seed yet. I haven't ploughed the ground'.

What are the implications of this line of thought? First, we shall need to know much more about the people whom we seek to reach with the gospel than we often do. Who are they? Why do they live where they live, and do what they do? What is their life-style, and which criteria determine it? What really matters to them? We have had people majoring on the message and minoring on the hearers. We have had people majoring on the hearers but minoring on the message. We need evangelists who major on both.

Then we shall need to ask at which points the gospel is likely to be meaningful to them. What is likely to draw them to the light or cause them to be uneasy about their darkness? What is it in our message which links with their moments of hope and resolution and confirms their times of inability and weakness? In what areas does their conscience seem to operate? Both deeds and words fit in here. Both the quality of our lives and the intelligibility of our language become equally necessary.

Thirdly, although Wesley eschewed proofs of God (a stance possibly supported by the religious and cultural settings in which he worked) may we not have to encourage those outside to discover those points of depth in life which are what Peter Berger calls 'Signals of Transcendance', or what Ian Ramsey called 'Disclosure Situations'—moments or experiences or attitudes which are common to human life, and yet which require more than a natural explanation if they are to have full meaning?

Fourthly, and most difficult of all, we may have to recognize that prevenient grace will begin to operate for some of our fellows, not in an immediate sense of the presence of God; but rather in a willingness to believe that life is deep, has meaning, is worthwhile. It may seem a long way back from our point of view; but if it is where people are then this is where we must begin. The dawning of that earliest light may send enough of a beam to shine the way towards God. But where are the christians—writers, broadcasters, actors, musicians, evangelists (plus neighbours, workmates and relatives) who are willing and able to co-operate with prevenient grace, so far back? And will it be attempted, as in my judgment it must, by those who, however far back they have to begin, are determined to lead people all the way to the feet of Christ?

The second of the areas of Wesleyan theology concerns his view of authority in religion. That the Bible stood at the centre of his sources is clear. In that sense he was, as he claimed, 'a man of one book'. It is equally clear that he was a man of one book only in the sense that the Bible had an authority for him over and above all other books. Witness his own prodigious reading, and his requirements of the clergy (see his Address to the Clergy 1756, *Works, vol. X,* pp. 480 ff.).

Wesley expects the clergyman to have a knowledge of his own office, of scripture, of original tongues (that is, those in which the Bible is written), of profane history, customs, chronology and geography, of sciences and above all logic, of metaphysics, of geometry, of the fathers (especially pre-Nicene) and of the world, by which he means men, maxims, tempers and manners. He also looks for common sense and good breeding—and deals with scorn with a statement he quotes; 'The boy, if he is fit for nothing else, will do well enough for a parson'. Thus he says we get 'dull, heavy, blockish ministers, with poor memories, defective in understanding and apprehension; incapable of reasoning or passing judgment'. He goes on, 'a blockhead may do well as soldier, tradesman, sailor, lawyer or physician, but O! think not of his being a minister . . .'.

His Christian Library, begun in 1749, with its fifty volumes culled from the world's classics in 'practical divinity'; his curriculum for the pupils at Kingswood School (see A. G. Ives, *Kingswood School in Wesley's Day and Since*, Epworth Press, 1970, pp. 11 ff.); and his demands of his own preachers, all show how widely he drew upon written sources of knowledge. The Bible was at the centre; but it was the centre of many other books. There are two implications which need to be taken with very great seriousness at this point. The first is, that in days when we are justly glad about the charismatic renewal of emphasis upon experience, an emphasis which ought to be easily recognized by Methodists, there is also need for deep intellectual rootage of the faith. Criteria for judging our experiences are as necessary as having the experiences themselves. The second is that in days when people outside the church begin to turn to us, however slightly, it is necessary for us to be sure that our response has a proper base in knowledge and understanding. There is no ground in Christianity for the rejection of true knowledge.

We must also remind ourselves that Wesley read the Bible at different levels. There is the 'literal' meaning, which is the foundation for the 'spiritual' meaning. The exegete searching for the literal meaning will require skill in a variety of disciplines, set out in his 'Address to the Clergy 1756', (*Works of John Wesley* vol. X, pp. 480 ff.). There will also be the need to 'deduce the proper corollaries, speculative and practical, from each text (ibid., p. 483). The preacher must, in addition, solve difficulties, answer objections and make suitable application to the consciences of his hearers (ibid., p. 491). Yet all along he has the highest view of Scripture, its inspiration, trustworthiness and authority. To Henry Venn he wrote, 'I believe all the Bible as far as I understand it. If I am a heretic, I became such by reading the Bible.' The 'analogy of faith' delivers him from being a literalist, but the Bible is at the heart of it all.

Of course, as a member and priest of the Church of England he was familiar with, and accepted, other sources of authority alongside that of the Bible. In particular he accepted the other two propounded by Richard Hooker, namely tradition and reason. But whereas Hooker appears to hold all three as of equal importance, each 'coming into its own' at certain points and over particular issues, Wesley constantly places Scripture above the other two.

What is more, he adds a fourth, experience. The fear of fanaticism ('enthusiasm' in eighteenth-century language) was both evident and justifiable among his contemporaries, in view of the previous century's political history. Yet Wesley was brought to a point where experience too became a source of authority. Bishop Butler of Bristol, in the now famous interview of Wesley, had perceived that, 'Sir, the pretending to extraordinary revelation and gifts of the Holy Ghost is a horrid thing, a very horrid thing'. As Bishop Moorman comments, 'Most of his fellow bishops would have concurred in this judgment' (*A History of the Church in England*, p. 281). Wesley's Aldersgate *experience* had meant too much for him to turn his back on the authority vested therein.

I marvel at the contrast between Wesley's letter, written to his father refusing the latter's pressure to succeed him at Epworth, with some twenty-six reasons why he should not accept, and the relentless preaching travelling in the triangle of hardship and difficulty which took him a quarter of a million miles and through forty thousand sermons. The difference between the rather pampered and spoilt scholar of the letter, and the committed evangelist of the second, is partly explicable in terms of the importance of experience to Wesley, and particularly the experience of Aldersgate Street. Aldersgate Street should not be seen as so important as to distract from other experiences, as for example in 1725 and his question about ordination. But it does offer a very important clue to the attachment of a source of authority to experience in Wesley's thinking. Yet even here Scripture must be supreme. So in his letter to Thomas Whitehead (probably) of 10 February 1748, concerning Quakerism, he writes, 'The Scriptures are the touchstone whereby Christians examine all, real or supposed revelations' (*The Letters of John Wesley*, II, p. 117).

It has often seemed to me that Wesley's views of authority

can be likened to a mobile. At the centre, around which all else circulates, is the Bible. Tradition, Reason and Experience are the other three elements in the mobile, each of them circulating around the Bible. Depending on one's position, or the mobile's circulation, one views the Bible via one or more of the other three, and the position one occupies is viewed from the Bible via one or more of the three. We are thus in a fixed relationship as between the importance of the Bible to the other three. Yet we are also in a flexible relationship of all four to the current situation. This combination of fixity and flexibility enabled Wesley to face his critics and his circumstances with a fair degree of consistency and a high potential for variety, depending upon the setting.

Does this still provide for us a way forward, internally to Methodism and ecumenically to the rest of the Church? Too often one or other figure in the mobile has been championed to the exclusion of the others. The history of the Church tells the sad story. Latterly, in terms of the last century, we have seen each of the other figures emphasized at the expense of the central one, Scripture. In reaction we have had Scripture so defended that the others were by implication unimportant or unnecessary. Have we now, in Methodism and ecumenically, reached a point where all can affirm the centrality of the Scriptures (though perhaps still differing about matters of inspiration and interpretation), while also acknowledging the vital, though supportive and interpretative role of the other three? And may we find unity in exploring the different ways in which we view the Scriptures, and the Scriptures view us, according to our varied circumstance, vantage point and need? This way we might discover far more in common on the one hand, yet a much richer variety of truth on the other, because we are all held within the orbit of the one mobile.

The third area of Wesleyan thought to which I now wish to turn is the concept of movement within the christian life. We noted earlier that Wesley's doctrine of sin was determinative for much of what followed. It also determines the character as well as the detail. Since sin breaks both man's relationship *with* God and his image *of* God, then salvation must restore both. Prevenient grace brings man to repentance, then follows justifying faith. New birth and justification are distinguished theoretically, but not in terms of time. The latter restores the relationship to God: the former begins the restoration of the image of God, leading on to sanctification and perfect love. Assurance is a possibility for all believers, though Wesley came to see that not all have it and that salvation does not depend upon it. Ultimately there is glorification.

The two major characteristics of this 'system' are first, the *orderliness* of it and second, the *movement* of it. It is *orderly* in that Wesley seems to know where a person is and ought to be at any given point. It is *moving* in that the aim is the restoration of the image of God in man. Nothing less will do, and as much as possible is to be achieved in this life. Wesley does not share the Lutheran fear that too much emphasis beyond justification will detract from salvation by faith alone, or from the all-sufficiency of Christ's saving work. Even sanctification is, according to Wesley, by faith. And all depends always upon the atonement wrought by Christ, its central effect being pardon. The combination of orderliness and movement lies close to the secret of Methodism's early development. The believers knew they were going somewhere experientially, and they knew where they were going. The hymns of Charles Wesley, and the sermons and writings of John pointed the way. The bands and classes enabled them to share the journey, sustained by the means of grace. Maybe the most striking characteristic about the early Methodists was not that the majority of them claimed to be perfected in love, but that the majority of them were seeking to be so perfected.

The Christian Church in our century has been through a series of onslaughts of such fierceness that to have survived at all is in itself a considerable achievement. The inner questioning about the nature and authority of the Bible, about the intellectual integrity of christian theology, about the validity of christian experience, about the relevance of christian faith have all been matched in the western world by an increasing tendency to seek satisfaction elsewhere and to discount the christian solutions to life's problems.

The result, not too surprisingly, has been one of fragmentation. Passages of Scripture have become treated as unauthoritative or simply wrong, elements in doctrinal belief have been dropped, experience has become suspect, faith treated as an optional extra. As a result the significance of preaching has often been discounted; the teaching of 'the faith' discontinued, and systems of theology viewed as imprisoning to the spirit and inhibiting to the mind.

A greater sense of freedom has undoubtedly been the legacy of such an approach. Unhelpful and irrelevant attitudes have also been revealed and discarded. The pioneers and explorers of the faith have been let loose in a world of discovery and knowledge.

But there is another side to the story too. Our excitement has often been gained at the expense of continuity. Our freedom has at times become license. Our passion for relevance has led us to discard timeless truths because our culture saw no value in them at the time. Occasionally we have simply been overwhelmed by the cleverness of unbelievers, or overimpressed by the brazen strength of modern cultural forms and expressions. Worst of all our believing and understanding have become fragmented. It is more like a bag of marbles than a bunch of grapes. We often lack a sense of direction because there are few links or clues to lead us on to the next point. Without a coherent system we find it difficult to assess new ideas or properly to assimilate new knowledge. It is not easy, either, to build a coherent life-style upon a fragmented belief system. Nor are apologetic and evangelism very confident in such circumstances. The motor car we have produced looks from some angles to be well-fitted for our twentieth century world. The only fears about it are whether the drivers have any sense of direction, and more seriously, whether it possesses an engine.

Has the Church now reached a point where it has weathered the storms of criticism from within and without, the onslaughts of pure, applied and behavioural sciences, of neglect from outside and uncertainty from within? If so, may we Methodists not rediscover a ready-made system; but the concept of the christian life understood as divine activity in human life, an activity characterized by a constant provision of grace enough for each new challenge, responded to by faith together with a deeper understanding of and experience of divine love transforming the life? Are we able again to be clear about an order of salvation, so that people know where they begin, how they move on, what they are progressing towards and when they have arrived? Is the challenge to perfect love, understood as a personality totally dominated by the love of God, so that mathematical concepts of sin and grace become irrelevant and unnecessary, not still desperately needed by our world? And is the Wesleyan balance of means of grace, intimate fellowship, service and evangelism, not still a pattern to follow in that direction? Until order and movement are again inserted into our concept of christian experience we may find that all our exhortation about better worship, deeper service in the world, more effective outreach will produce disappointing results. Jesus' parable of the two houses on different foundations is perhaps relevant here.

We come next to the combination of evangelistic fervour and social righteousness. Few are likely to miss the passion with which Wesley, in his own words, 'Offered Christ'. Perhaps the surprising thing is his capacity, alongside the frequent *declaration* of the gospel, to engage in *doing* the gospel. His last letter, written to William Wilberforce, was an encouragement to continue to the end the fight against the wicked practice of slavery. His educational endeavours—in schools and orphanages—were remarkably farsighted responses to the problems of children in his day. Some of his medical prescriptions may seem somewhat bizarre to us today. I do not know many Methodist men, for example, who rub onions onto their heads to cure baldness. That may be why we have so many bald-headed Methodist men! His use of electrolysis is positively terrifying; his system of loans extremely practical. He twice expressed concern and did something for needy French prisoners of war in Knowle near Bristol, and himself collected in the streets in order to help the poor.

One has of course to remind oneself that eighteenth century England was much more sparsely populated than now. In that sense an outstanding person could influence large sections of the population. This was, as G. M. Trevelyan has reminded us, the last age in English history in which outstanding individuals could sway the entire nation (a judgment made before the media was exerting the power it has · today. I wonder what Trevelyan would think of that). Then the needs were only too striking and apparent. The solutions were largely obvious. And the structures of eighteenth century England were comparatively simple. Gerald Cragg estimated that something like forty families ruled the nation as a whole. There was, moreover, already the beginning of a move for better conditions of life; a move both encouraged and in some senses met by Wesley's message.

No matter how we plead the different circumstances, however, one thing seems to be plain. The early Methodists, and particularly the earliest Methodist, combined the passions of an evangelical faith and social righteousness in a quite remarkable way. The theological roots of such a combination are numerous. There is the conviction that genuine faith will be accompanied by evidences. There is the passion for holiness; holiness understood in practical terms, as seen in the importance attached to the Sermon on the Mount. And there is the goal of perfect love, combining the aim and a method of achieving it. What is more it was a way consistent with New Testament teaching and especially the example of Jesus himself. It is also an example which shames us. The problems *are* larger; but so are we. The situations *are* more complex; but so are our resources. It *is* harder for an individual to influence so many; but then our advanced organization should be able to help us to do things corporately to greater effect. The structures *have* proliferated, but so has our capacity to penetrate them. The question is whether we have the characteristically Methodist passion to do these things, and to face the consequences. Maybe the recent furore over the Programme to Combat Racism serves as a timely reminder of the pain which results when Christians face such problems with honesty. One makes this comment without, at this point, passing judgment on any of the responses to that programme which are evident among Christians today.

Even at this point we have not faced the heart of the problem. Methodism in general does engage in evangelism, and *is* socially and politically engaged. But have we the capacity or the concern to allow the two things not only to exist side-by-side in our lives but also to influence one another as they did in the one life of John Wesley! We are in danger of stopping short with statements of mutual admiration for one another. We have still to ask how social and political involvement leads to a making of new christians, or how our evangelization makes for a better world and changes structures. That task is only just beginning. Until it is accomplished we shall continue to divide by our preferences what God—as creator and redeemer—intends to stay together and relate to one another. In such a situation a fundamental wholeness is missing. Till our deeds create a curious audience our words fall on deaf ears. If our deeds are not followed by witness in word they fail to communicate the whole gospel. Let the 'doers' and the 'proclaimers' close ranks till they face the same way and can hear one another genuinely as they march into battle.

Lastly, and as a commentary on all the rest, there is Wesley's capacity to tolerate tension within his theology.

Rupert Davies, in his chapter on Methodist doctrine in the *History of the Methodist Church in Great Britain,* Vol. I (Epworth Press, 1965, pp. 147–8) claims that Wesley is not a *creative* theologian in the sense of one who by his incisive thinking inaugurates a new era of theological insight. Nor, says Davies, was he a systematic theologian in terms of writing a Summa Theologica or an Institutes of Religion. Yet, he goes on, Wesley rendered great service by selecting an area of theology he believed to be neglected, and by showing himself in that area of personal salvation to be truly a systematic theologian (op. cit., p. 14).

I would simply wish to add the suggestion that Wesley's greatest contribution of all was his ability to face seemingly intractable problems and to place the various possibilities into a creative tension which was not resolved but was life-giving. Thus a Protestant soteriology is placed alongside a Catholic doctrine of perfection. The clue here as we have seen, is prevenient grace. He holds to a doctrine of perfection which tolerates elements needing atonement yet not properly viewed as sin. The key to this tension is that its highest point is divine love overwhelming a human life. The individual inner experience of salvation and the corporate sacramental commitment are held together by an unusually comprehensive view of the means of grace. He affirms a doctrine of assurance alongside an exhortation to live in hope, because he accepts that a believer can fall away. So assurance is assurance of present salvation. He sees salvation as by grace through faith alone, yet stresses works as a vital part of the christian life. The clue is that the works are 'evidences'. They are *our* works, but only because the Spirit of God, restoring the image of God in us, works the works through us. He places crisis experiences alongside process experiences, because he observes the Spirit enabling both in human life.

Is it too proud of us to feel that we may have here a theological method which we can share with the rest of Christendom? In so doing we should not be claiming that *we only* have discovered these things. But we might with justification claim that because Wesley eschewed speculative theology and other ranges of the religious mind he might well have scaled; because he did so on a basis of Scripture seen in the light of and shedding light upon Tradition, Reason and Experience; and because at heart he was an evangelist and teacher of the love of God, we can confidently call all our brothers and sisters in Christ to join us in standing back a little further from our mutual tensions to discover whether there may not be at each point a third way, embracing the two previously seen as exclusive, by reason of some other insight equally biblical and well-founded. Or maybe we shall at points have simply to affirm a paradox, realizing as Wesley did, that while a paradox may be frustrating, it can nevertheless be the basis of invigorating and authentic Christian believing and living. This may yet prove to be our greatest jewel—a way of doing theology—which we can gladly place alongside the treasures we thankfully receive from others.

# CHAPTER NINE

# The Charismatic Renewal in Methodism

*Address at the Renewal Conference,*
*Cliff College, Derbyshire*
*12 July 1978*

How naturally does Charismatic teaching find a home in Methodism? Dr Leslie Davison in *Pathway to Power*, and more recently and specifically Dr Bill Davies, in *Spirit Baptism and Spiritual Gifts in Early Methodism,* have looked at aspects of this question. Plainly if the ethos of Methodism is right then the problem of separation will be a much smaller one.

In terms of the teaching and practice of John Wesley himself, and of the Methodist Revival as a whole, the signs are not too favourable, especially if one is looking for commendatory teaching and records of charismatic activity described and accounted for in terms now made familiar by classical and neo-Pentecostalism. Some words of Dr Davison, quoted by Dr Davies, well illustrate the dilemma presented by the evidence:

'It could well be that because the first Methodists did not expect to receive the charismata, and indeed did not particularly want them, that they created a mental or spiritual block to their reception' (Davies, p. 1 from *Pathway to Power*, p. 73).

Dr Davies is not sure that they did not want them, and he notes that the Spirit is not always limited by what we want. He seeks to discern the presence of the charismata even where they were not so described. He also shows that the setting, with criticisms of enthusiasm, was not favourable for claims about charismata or their exercise, and that Wesley modified an earlier view and came to believe that the gifts seen in the early church were withdrawn because of unbelief and hardness. There *are* a number of ways, however, in which the charismatic can claim a very close link between Methodism and his experience and teaching.

Historically it seems clear that there is a direct link between Wesley's teaching on sanctification and the beginnings of the Pentecostal Movement in the twentieth century. That link is via the nineteenth century Holiness Movements, who seized on aspects of Wesley's teaching, particularly that of a second experience subsequent to conversion, and instantaneous in character. In particular Charles G. Finney linked Holiness Theology from Methodism with revivalist techniques, but called the second experience a baptism in the Holy Spirit. As Bruner comments:

'From Methodism through American revivalism and the person and work of Charles Finney (the institutionalizer of revivalism) the line is a straight one that leads through the holiness movement directly into Pentecostalism'.[1]

Secondly, we may note that there were some Methodist ministers at the heart of a number of the new departures out of which Pentecostalism grew—Parham in Kansas and Texas, Barrat in Scandinavia and England, Pastor W. C. Hoover in

[1] F. D. Bruner, *A Theology of the Holy Spirit* (Hodder and Stoughton, 1971).

Chile. There is here the significant point that our religious background not only enables us to recognize what is now present from our experience, it also helps us to feel what is lacking. What those men—as Methodists—felt to be lacking, their Pentecostal experience supplied.

Thirdly, there is the theological and experiential point alluded to above, namely Wesley's stress upon a second experience; albeit in relation to sanctification. This needs much elucidation in terms of crisis and growth, but *both* are present in Wesley.

Fourthly, we must not underestimate the requirement in Wesley's teaching of evidences to substantiate any claim to religious experience. It was this which brought him from time to time under the accusation of teaching salvation by works, but it also preserved his followers in face of the danger of false claims and fanaticism. It also, however, harmonizes well with the Pentecostal refusal of a baptism merely received by faith, without evidence (e.g. tongues), and it is interesting to hear a modern Methodist Charismatic leader speaking of 'The primacy of intimate personal experience of the Lord, with evidences, . . . as central to the Holy Spirit's work in the believer'.[2] The detail of evidences required is different, but the principle is the same.

Fifthly, the theological emphasis in Wesley's teaching on salvation is also relevant here. Part of the criticism of the whole Pentecostal movement, whether classical or neo-, is that it moves the point of emphasis away from Justification by Faith and the New Birth, where Christ's work is so central, and moves it on to a future experience subsequent to the New Birth, thus devaluing Christ's atoning work, and also the centre piece of Salvation by Grace through Faith. As Hollenweger writes about Pentecostal teaching, 'the doctrine of justification is emptied of meaning and reduced to a preliminary stage for beginners in Christianity' (*The Pentecostals*, p. .

---

[2] See also Tom Smails' *Reflected Glory*, p. 33. c.f. Wesley re. the Church, *Works of John Wesley*, vol. VI, p. 400, Sermon 74 'Of the Church'.

329). There can be little doubt that Wesley would have taken issue with this criticism, since for him the restoration of the lost image of God in man was so uppermost that justification must enable him to press on to sanctification and perfect love without any devaluation of Christ's work, since He was honoured throughout. He would have warmed, no doubt, to the recent editorial of *Dunamis* (No. 7, April 1974). 'At no point would one want however to give the Spirit priority over and above Jesus. It is to Jesus we look for the beginning (author) and the end (perfector) of all our faith' (p. 38). One can't help feeling that Wesley would stand with the pentecostals of every hue and against their critics on this point.

Sixthly, and allied to the previous section, there is Wesley's optimism of grace, with its glad openness to all that God has for the believer, and a refusal to limit the promises of God or their fulfilment in human life, either because of the sinfulness of human nature or because of realism about the world and how things happen in it. There is much here that finds response in the charismatics and their outlook.

Seventhly, there is Wesley's concern for the witness of the Spirit, personally experienced, with all its subsequent events. It is no coincidence that Davies and Peart find this to be the closest Methodist analogy to what they are trying to describe by baptism in the Spirit (Occasional Paper, pp. 15 ff.). And so did Dr Davison, (*Pathway to Power*, p. 60). Note here how we find the models for our descriptions in the materials of our past.

Eighthly, there is the way in which, as Rupert Davies has pointed out, Wesley selected from the whole range of theological thought the area of personal salvation as his centre of emphasis, albeit with practical, corporate and social outworking. This is the level at which most ordinary people operate.

The aim of the above excursion has not been to demonstrate, in a simplistic way, that since there is some harmony with Wesley's teaching, therefore charismatic teaching is necessarily to be welcomed or ought to be central in our Methodist teaching today. We do well to be warned by Dr John Kent's introductory comments in *The Age of Disunity* (Epworth, 1966, p. ix) that on the one side there is a remarkable lack in early Methodism of phenomena one associates with Pentecostalism, and that on the other Methodism might well be called a 'Holiness Revival manqué', since as a holiness movement it virtually died in the 1760s. Neither have we shown the elements in Wesley's teaching which would be an obstacle to some forms of charismatic emphasis; his great stress upon the use of reason, for example. Nor must we assume that the present-day Methodist Church does or should stand in the same position. But there is surely enough to show that the charismatics have much in our title deeds to which they can legitimately appeal in their experience and their teaching, whether or not Mr Wesley taught or claimed baptism in the Spirit.

Leaving history behind us we may now enquire about the strengths and positive contributions of the contemporary Charismatic Movement. We begin with the word 'liberation'. Through the movement there is a joyous acceptance of genuine Christian qualities—joy, peace and power, for example—not by a grim striving, but as the result of the Spirit's influence. The same is true about personal witness. People who have not been able to speak about their faith find themselves freed to tell others. In this setting, concern about the doctrine of the Holy Spirit is not that which must complete some theological system, but out of necessity to formulate a framework which will adequately cover the experienced reality of the Christian faith.

Next we must note the 'enabling' which is involved. The movement does not confuse the gift of the Spirit with the manifestations which follow, but manifestations there are. In particular there is the rediscovery of the so-called 'extraordinary' gifts of the Spirit, gifts such as speaking with tongues, interpreting tongues, and prophecy. Charismatics in general are not tied, as one might fear they would be, either to an order of priority among the gifts, or to a particular set of gifts. Ministry, celibacy and martyrdom are all included in the gifts involved. Nor are the 'extra-ordinary' gifts elevated above others, except in the sense that they receive stress because they do seem to have been neglected by many parts of the church for a long time. Much more striking, however, is the associated idea that all of life is a gift, and the consequent attitude of thankfulness so clearly revealed in the movement itself.

Next comes the concept and experience of 'sharing'. This has become a vital part of the activities, and there are significant features involved. One is the spirit of love and mutual concern noticed by visitors to such groups. The second is the largely unprepared nature of the proceedings; there being a real attempt to wait upon the leading of the Spirit, and a willingness to allow anyone to lead as he or she is led. Then there is the naturalness of the proceedings, whether there is talk or not. And the freedom apparently felt by all to take part as they are led. There is also the mutual inter-relationship of the Spirit's gifts, the tongue speaker upon the interpreter, the prophet upon the fellowship of discernment, and so on. It is this experience of sharing which leads to the phrase 'body ministry', and which helps to save the movement from being too individualistic in tone and emphasis.

Then there is the new experience in 'worship'. That there is an interest and concern would be expected where tongues are involved. Yet excitement is not a note that is often struck by commentators. Reverence certainly is, and so is the element of praise. Far more praise is heard than in more usual worship, where petition and intercession play such a part. The note of thankfulness pervades much of charismatic worship.

Another aspect prominent in the testimonies of charismatic ministers is the renewal of power in their preaching, and in the desire to preach.

A difference is felt, too, in 'private devotion'. The sense of meaning in Bible reading, the enjoyment of prayer, and the new love of Christ provide moving testimony to the changed experience of many charismatics.

Arising from some of the above emphases, yet not wholly covered by them, is the understanding and experience of the 'priesthood of all believers'. At the level of worship, of group meeting and of personal encounter, a new factor has entered the relationship between lay and ordained, namely the consideration of gifts and their exercise.

So much for the strengths. Many christians who do not belong to the movement in any formal way have been helped by such emphases to a richer personal experience. But are there any weaknesses?

It is probably worth introducing this section with a necessary distinction between the validity of a man's experience and the accuracy with which he describes it, or finds biblical and theological defences for it. We need to be clear that to criticize some of the description and the foundations advanced is not necessarily to discount the experience itself.

This leads naturally to the first point, namely to question the expression 'baptism in the Spirit' and the attempt to make it a second experience necessary to the full Christian life. I will note the following:

(a) The use of the Acts of the Apostles as the basis for doctrinal systems, as Pentecostalism of any kind needs to do, is a doubtful procedure if support of a fairly solid kind is not forthcoming from other sources.

(b) It is difficult to find anywhere in the gospels teaching about a two-stage experience.

(c) More surprising still is its absence from the epistles, evidently intended to teach the young churches and, on pentecostal or charismatic presuppositions, surely likely to lay great stress on this necessary second experience. Yet as both Salisbury *The Holy Spirit Experience*[3] and Bridge and

[3] Lutterworth, 1973

Phypers *Spiritual Gifts and the Church*[4] show, there is no single case which requires such interpretation.

As J. G. D. Dunn in *Baptism in the Holy Spirit*[5] has argued, Baptism in the Spirit, in Biblical terms, is that which makes a man a Christian; that is, it is part of his initial entry into the faith, not a later completion of his experience. He writes, 'to be baptized in the Holy Spirit' is 'never directly associated with the promise of power (in the New Testament) but is always associated with entry into the Messianic Age or the Body of Christ'.[6]

Secondly, there is the danger that what may be a genuine *part* of the Christian faith and practice could become the whole faith and practice for some, especially young people entering the faith via charismatic experience. This is partly accounted for by the striking nature of the gifts involved, and partly by the previous neglect of these in the church. But it becomes serious as a criticism in two different areas.

There is the danger of narrowing down the *doctrine* of the Holy Spirit in the interests of emphasizing His *work* in the life of the believer. While leaders of the Movement in Methodism assert their conviction over a wider range, the Movement has not yet adequately related concepts of individual baptizing and empowering by the Spirit to those of His work in Creation, Society and History. Until this is done there will always be a tendency towards narrowness of an unhelpful kind, and towards an inward-looking framework for understanding the Spirit's work.

There is also the danger, inherent in all teaching which encourages, or even allows for, a second experience after New Birth, of undervaluing the initial experience and the regular growth that is part of the everyday experience of the Christian. This is not so much a point about whether Jesus is neglected in the interests of the Holy Spirit, but rather

[4] Inter-varsity Press, 1973.
[5] S. C. M. 1970.
[6] Dunn, J. G. D., *Baptism in the Holy Spirit*, p. 228.

the normal processes of God's dealings with His people are being set on one side in the interests of what one might kindly call 'abnormal' ways. Where people, and particularly young people, enter Christianity via the Charismatic movement which is self-conscious about its special role, rather than via the normal life of a local church, this danger would seem to be increased.

In the third place one has to pause for one moment over the weaknesses attendant upon all Christian movements stressing what might be called the higher Christian life, over against the somewhat humdrum standard accepted by most Christians. 'And shall we ever live at this poor dying rate?' has been a proper question for Christians to ask, lest we become lulled into very second-rate estimates of what the Christian life is about, when God has much better things for us. But there are attendant dangers, too, as all such movements have found. Especially there is danger of hypocrisy, pretence, exaggeration, increasing the distinction for effect.

Closely associated with the previous point, and hinted at there, is the need to safeguard the place of the mind in the Christian life. Sometimes people say 'God told me' without exploring criteria for determining a 'word from the Lord'. When one is involved in a movement which highlights a gift or gifts which seem to by-pass the mind, or at least allocate to it a fairly subsidiary role, one has to prepare a warning signal about the dangers of proceeding to neglect it increasingly, in the interests of direct communications from God which remove the necessity for hard thought and careful planning. We need to ponder the words of the American Bishop Hughes who said that 'too many people are using the Holy Spirit as a labour-saving device'.

Next there is the question of adequate awareness of sociological and psychological factors which are at work in the spiritual growth of all Christians. For example, the 'instant truth' of television interviews is a dangerous factor. It is not just our religious, psychological and social setting, but our general setting too which pushes us towards easy solutions to difficult problems.

It is not enough simply to establish historical links, affirm strengths and indicate weaknesses. One must now ask—without presumption—what tasks are still faced by the Charismatic Movement and by the Christian Church at large in the light of the evidence set out above.

One of the recurring enigmas of church history has been the potential of spiritual revivals for dividing the church. Methodism is itself an example of the syndrome. And in each case there are faults on both sides. Take, for example, the celebrated confrontation between John Wesley and the Bishop of Bristol, Bishop Butler. The concentration so easily focuses upon what the initiates of the new experience are gaining by it, and what the rest are resenting about it. In our Methodist origins, individual experience, band and class meetings, lay preachers, extempore prayer were all centres of such controversy.

I would suggest that what is needed in such situations is to avoid such divisive centres of concentration, and to find common challenges, the facing of which will require the available resources of all those involved, and will provide a more rigorous setting for a discovery by each of the others' genuine sources of inspiration, experience and judgment.

In order to put this thesis to the test I suggest a number of such possible points of advance.

There is great need for the Church to explore the flexibility and diversity of ministries within her ranks, alongside a flexible and diverse ordained ministry. The Charismatic Movement is not by any means the first in this century to high-light this need. The emergence of team ministries, with a limited role for each member, has done so. And the development of so-called sector ministries (such ministers are now known as 'ministers in other appointments') with its increased freedom from church structures, has added another pressure in this direction. Some evangelicals are feeling the need for full-time ordained evangelists. There is the development, described by A. E. Harvey in his book *Priest or President* whereby every previous preserve of ordained ministry has been invaded by the lay person—whether sacrament or preaching, counselling or pastoral visitation, leadership or administration.

Nevertheless, the charismatic insight and practice concerning 'body ministry' is striking a serious blow at the pattern of ordained ministry with which the churches in England have long been familiar. If ministry is tied more to gift and function than to status and authorization, how is the role of ordained ministry to be defined? If group ministry rather than individual ministry becomes the practice, where does the ordained minister stand? If church structures still adhere to pyramidal models, with the ordained minister at the apex, how will it withstand the multiplication of vital spiritual power and roles at the base of the pyramid?

These are not exclusively charismatic problems. Nor are they exposed by charismatic emphases only. But the modern church, charismatic and non-charismatic, must face them, and all the resources available are needed to do so.

A second contemporary (though recurring) perplexity for christianity is the relationship between personal and institutional religion. Church historians can provide any enquirer with a list of celebrated cases of this perplexity in the history of the church, from Montanism through Methodism to the so-called para-churches of today.

Again, the Charismatic Movement has high-lighted the problem in its own way, but was not the first in our time to do so. Nor is it a specifically 'charismatic' problem. Most of the early breakaways from Wesleyan Methodism were due to the 'centre versus circumference' kind of ecclesiastical dispute. The Jesus Kids were in our time another form of the same tension. So, I would judge, are the Ashram communities. The apparent 'organizational' stage of any revival movement so often seems to be the harbinger of its decline in spiritual power. The growth of house churches today may be partly due to the conviction that institutional religion is dead or moribund religion.

The question is much deeper than it appears, however. At root it is, like all problems, a theological one. Put bluntly, it is the question, 'Can a religion based on incarnation avoid institutional form for any length of time?' History, with its procession of secessionist groups which either fade out or end up more highly organized than their parent body, would seem to demand a negative response to the question put in that form. A more positive approach, at theological level, is to ask how 'Incarnation and Redemption' can live harmoniously together in the life of the church. It is not a 'charismatic', nor a 'non-charismatic' question; it is a question for all christians to face, and we will only properly face it together. As we do so we shall begin truly to understand one another.

There is in the third place the need for christian balance about beginning and continuing in the christian faith. Put more sharply it has to do with what is the fundamental dividing line in life. Christians have often needed to be reminded, as non-christians need to be told, that the distinction is not between life and death, but between being in Christ or out of Christ. In many forms, however, christians have often denied this in practice, from the divisions in Corinth through to the present day. We find ways of excluding one another from the group—ours of course—which is in our judgment at the very centre of what God is doing. There is the scholarly in-group, the sacramentalist clique, the liberal clientele, the radical cadre, the conservative camp, the activist party and now the charismatic body meeting. None of us actually says that the others are inferior christians. Some of us affirm that they are not. Some go even further and protest that they are better than we are, really. . . . Yet built into our actions and words, our testimony and conversation, there is enough to communicate that we are first class travellers, and that there is only one such compartment on the gospel train.

This is serious—quite apart from the divisive effect on the

Church—for two quite separate reasons. One is that it separates by selection what ought to be kept together. The other is that it denies the one essential element of the christian life, which is that we are saved by grace through faith. Lutheran criticism of Pentecostalism (as exemplified by F. D. Bruner *A Theology of the Holy Spirit*) is particularly trenchant here.

Of course we must protest that some christians *do* have deeper insights into their faith than others; that some *are* more committed, that some *are* better witnesses. But which of us wishes to argue that all the 'better Christians' belong to his group, except by first isolating himself and his group from all others so that the evidence won't be available to himself or them?

We need to find a way of affirming every genuine gift of God, every authentic insight, every legitimate Christian life style, without losing the integrity of our own. For christians to meet inter-denominationally because of a shared conviction—of theology or liturgy, of churchmanship or charity, of action or experience—is a helpful starting point. But it can never be a terminus, because it may simply serve to harden the isolation of each of those groups within its own denomination. And this is a problem we *all* face.

There is fourthly the question of alternatives which are really complimentary to one another. One need only mention them for the point to be made. There is evangelism and service, salvation of individuals and reform of structures, christian experience as joyful victory or persevering humiliation, worship as exciting fulfilment or faithfulness to tradition. The list does not end there. For a variety of reasons, however, we tend to select what we like, or what we consider priority, to the exclusion of the rest. Yet the wholeness of christian experience requires them all, and all are found in the biblical foundations and the living tradition of the christian community. And it is not just your problem or mine—it is a common christian problem.

In closing I make two observations. The first is that every

now and again in the history of the Church a moment arrives when, through certain people, movements or circumstances, we are given by God an opportunity to discover and demonstrate something to be possible which was not previously thought to be possible. Such a moment in time becomes a signal moment, a moment after which history is never the same because something of great significance has taken place. I believe the Charismatic Movement in the Christian Church today to be situated at such a moment. And the signal element is not the renewed experience of the Spirit which lies at its heart. The signal element will be the spread of the insights gained throughout all the denominations, and the containing of those insights within such denominations without schism. That it will be too powerful to be contained without change I readily accept. This is why I have explored the four areas above. But that it should renew and revive the present groups of christians will be the real test of a signal moment of grace.

My second observation is, therefore, that we are on the edge of such a moment. We have not yet arrived there. My fear for charismatics is that they may settle for what they have (which is, after all, what all christians could have had in any age since Pentecost) instead of pressing on through all the tribulation and glory of being part of the new thing I believe God is seeking to do. And that is renewal without division, revival without schism, blessing of a part which becomes blessing for the whole.

Whether or not this modern miracle takes place is not entirely up to any one of us, even humanly speaking. But humanly speaking we *can* do a great deal to facilitate it. For that I pray.

# III

## *MISSION*

CHAPTER TEN

# Biblical Roots of Compassionate Service

*Address at the Convocation of the Wesley Deaconess Order,*
*Tunstall*
*27 April 1979*

THE subject before us is a very extensive one, and will inevitably, in the space available, be reduced to '*Some* Biblical Roots . . .'. It is much too important an element in the christian life to be exhausted in such a short study.

**The Setting**
The setting for our study is extremely favourable. The Free Churches, along with all other christian bodies, can now take heart from three documents which each refer extensively to the topic of this address. The Lausanne Covenant (1974), reflecting wide-spread evangelical conviction; the Nairobi Report (1975), representing the World Council of Churches; and the Apostolic Exhortation of Pope Paul VI, 'Evangelization in the Modern World' (1975), on behalf of the Roman Catholic Church, all showed deep concern about the quality of our service in the world as part of our mission. We therefore join a

much larger body of christians as we apply ourselves to this topic.

## God's Nature

We begin with *the nature of God*. The basic stimulus towards loving service is not the need of the needy but the nature of God. He provides for the needs of his creatures (Genesis 1–2) and sets his love on his chosen people because it is his nature to do so (Deuteronomy 7:6–8, including 'the Lord set his love upon you . . . because the Lord loves you'). He loves because he loves. In Hosea 11, surely one of the most moving passages in all Scripture, he loves in spite of his people's unfaithfulness. 'How can I give you up, O Ephraim. How can I hand you over, O Israel . . . My heart recoils within me, my compassion grows warm and tender' (verse 8). In Matthew 6:25–33 Jesus assures his hearers that they need not be consumed with anxiety about their physical needs, for the God who cares for the birds, the lilies, the grass, knows what they need, and will see that they receive it. God's concern for his world is summed up in John 3:16 in terms of his love expressed in Jesus Christ's provision of a way of salvation, which Paul works out in Romans 5:6–11. God's love is shown in Christ's death, not for worthy people, but for sinners. 1 John 4:7–21 picks up the same theme, affirming that love is of the essence of God's nature, and that the supreme expression of that love was the sending of his Son for our sins.

This selection of representative passages from a variety of biblical writers underlines the extreme importance of beginning in the right place. If christians engage in compassionate service it is because their God is like that. The implications of such an affirmation deserve careful attention.

## Implications

The first is that the major root of compassionate service is a *theological* one in the fundamental sense of that word. 'Theology' is the knowledge of God. We are not called to engage in compassionate service because such behaviour enhances our image in the world (though it does). Nor is it in order to attract others into the kingdom of God, (though it will). It is not even because the need of others moves us (though it should). It is because our God expresses his love by compassionate action towards his creatures and we—as his children—display the family likeness. (We will return to this later.)

The second implication of such a starting point is that our compassionate service *is not strictly speaking ours but his through us.* We do not (or ought not to) have our campaigns which we offer to him. He is constantly caring for the creatures he loves, and we are invited to join in his perfect caring for his world. This both puts us under greater pressure and yet relieves us of pressure. We are put under pressure because *our* standards of compassion and service will no longer suffice. That people should be living sub-human lives in a world in which full humanity was intended for all is to us a scandal. To God it is a blasphemy—a living denial of his nature and purpose for his world. For us to provide amelioration of circumstances for 'a reasonable proportion' of the needy, will be a source of gratitude and perhaps self-congratulation. God will not rest till *all* his creatures are properly cared for. To seek to be engaged in his mission of caring for the world is to be put under much greater pressure than we have as yet realized. The Creator's concern is with his entire creation. Our schemes look paltry against such a back-cloth.

Yet we are also relieved of pressure by such a consideration. Too much of our concern, planning and activity, has an element of the frantic and frenetic about it. We behave as though everything depended upon us. We need to be reminded that the theological root of all such work is the conviction that it is—originally and ultimately—God's responsibility, not ours. Maybe our people are weary because of the constant buffetings they receive at our hands about their duty to the needy and under-privileged. Perhaps they should hear more the assurance that God is concerned to meet such needs, and that he will provide the strength and the impetus for us to play our small part in his large purposes. To take God's responsibility for the world out of his hands is to be crushed by it.

The third implication is that worship and contemplation and study of God is not an alternative—still less a rival—to compassionate service. *It is its true source.* As our knowledge of God's being extends, and our response and submission to him deepen, we shall share in his compassion for the world and express it in our lives. Only as we are renewed in our vision of God shall we be quickened for service in the world. It is this vision, not the harrowing accounts of world need, which serve as the heart of our compassion. Our christian communicators may be spending too much time pointing us in the wrong direction.

The dichotomy between the pietist and activist in christian believing is a harmful one, essentially because it is a false one. Experience of God and service of one's neighbour go hand in hand, as our Lord himself pointed out so long ago (Luke 10:27, based on Deuteronomy 6:5 and Leviticus 19:18). It is interesting to notice that in the Leviticus passage this same process is reinforced—'You shall be . . . because I am', and that in the list of precepts enjoined upon the people, the words 'I am the Lord' are repeated fifteen times.

### The Prophets and Duty

The second root of compassionate service is well communicated by Old Testament prophets. Because God is a compassionate God we *not only may be compassionate, it is our duty to be so in our attitudes and our actions.* The words of Isaiah 1:12–17 should be read slowly and with great care as a regular spiritual exercise. Or we may take Isaiah 3:15, 'What do you mean by crushing my people, by grinding the face of the poor says the Lord God of hosts?' It is surely not without significance that the prophet responsible for such words was he who had a vision of God in the temple (Isaiah 6). Jeremiah is equally strong in his exhortations. 'Thus says the Lord: do justice and righteousness, and deliver from the hand of the oppressor him who has been robbed. And do no wrong or violence to the alien, the fatherless and the widow, nor shed innocent blood in this place' (Jeremiah 22:3). And there are the beautiful and haunting words of Amos 5:24, 'But let justice roll down like waters, and righteousness like an ever-flowing stream'.

The link between this and our first section is a truth I learned from J. N. Schofield in Cambridge many years ago, that the Old Testament prophets often operate like oarsmen, moving into the future with their backs towards it, their eyes fixed on what has been. The past provides them with the only criteria for determining how things are or ought to be, and how the future will turn out. They assume that the people of God will behave in a manner consonant with the nature of God, so their vision of who he is becomes a monitor of what his people should be. Since he is a just God, his people should be consumed with a passion for justice. Since he is righteous his people should be and do right. Since he cares for the needy, so should they. Isaiah 45:18–25 works this approach out powerfully, in the setting of a court hearing where God gives evidence in his defence. Because he is a creator God, there should be no chaos in his world (18–19). Because he is the only God and Saviour, there should be no idolatry (20–21). Because he is the Lord, there should be no rebellion (22–25).

**May or Must?**
We not only *may* reflect God's compassion on the needy; as his people we *must*. This is the message of the prophets. It is not a matter of choice but of obedience. Of course we must recognize that their concern was largely for the treatment of fellow-Jews, as was the Leviticus passage quoted earlier. The concept of the righteous nation is vital to their preaching. Yet

the logic of being the people of God is no less demanding upon us. We reveal the nature of the God we serve by the kind of life we seek to lead.

### John the Baptist

John the Baptist is in many ways the clue to the next step we must take in turning to the significance of Jesus and his ministry. John's ministry and message had much to do with preparing the way of the Lord. But what kind of way would be fitting? He quotes the prophets in his preaching (Mark 1:2–3 and parallels). He tells the people that their lives are not fit to receive the Lord. But his advice is on the one side to repent and be baptized for forgiveness, and on the other to live lives which demonstrated their new direction, sharing their coats and their food, treating others fairly, and being content (Luke 3:10–14). The vision of a just God and the exhortation to live accordingly reflect the burden of the prophets. In this way John brings us to Jesus.

The attempt to be selective about the meaning of Jesus Christ for our topic introduces the danger of simplifying the complex and distorting the picture. Yet certain aspects stand out clearly.

### The Meaning of Incarnation

The first is *the significance of the Incarnation* itself. Quite apart from what Jesus Christ said and did, suffered and achieved, we must treat with great seriousness the implications of his very existence. John 1:14 ('And the Word became flesh and dwelt among us, full of grace and truth; and we have beheld his glory, glory as of the only Son from the Father') was the late Professor William Barclay's favourite verse of Scripture because, among other things, it spells out God's willing involvement in and commitment to humanity, with all its sinfulness and need. And, we may add, it is commitment of a physical kind. It is true that 'here we have no lasting city' (Hebrews 13:14), but we should be saved from neglecting this life on the strength of such statements when we recall that God's supreme revelation of himself was in bodily form. We, who are what we are because God became involved, at cost, in the business of human living, can hardly follow Jesus Christ as disciples and at the same time draw back from costly involvement with the needs of others for whom he lived and died.

## People of the Kingdom

This brings us to a second implication of Jesus Christ for our study. He came announcing the kingdom of God (Mark 1:15). It is fascinating to observe who entered that kingdom, and which people benefited most from his ministry. *Many were the outcasts or under-privileged of society.* There were lepers (Mark 1:40–45; Luke 17:11–19), gentiles (Matthew 8:5–13; John 4:46–54), women and children (Matthew 8:14–17; 9:20–26; Luke 13:11–13; Mark 10:13–16) and notorious sinners (Matthew 11:19; 21:32; Mark 2:16–17; Luke 7:37–50; 15:1–2; 19:1–10). As Joachim Jeremias comments, his 'following consisted predominantly of the disreputable, the uneducated, the ignorant, whose religious ignorance and moral behaviour stood in the way of their access to salvation, according to the convictions of the time'. We may cherish the idea that all persons are equal in the sight of God; it is difficult, however, both in the Old Testament prophets and in the ministry of Jesus, to avoid the conclusion that the poor and needy are particularly precious to him.

## Teaching of the Kingdom

A third element relates not so much to the people of the kingdom as to the *teaching of the kingdom.* C. H. Dodd taught many of us to see the parables in this light, and of all the parables the most significant concerning compassionate service is that of the Good Samaritan (Luke 10:25–37). The simple command to the lawyer 'Go and do likewise' is not so simply put into action without understanding the meaning of the parable. The techniques of contrast and surprise often

*115*

point to the heart of the parables of Jesus. The contrast is clear. On the one side are the priest and the levite, with unquestionably acceptable religious pedigrees. On the other side is the Samaritan, instantly hated and rejected by Jesus' Jewish hearers on the strength of some six centuries of unhappy conflict. The surprise is that, of those two sides, it is the cursed Samaritan who goes to the aid of the man (presumably a Jew) on the roadside dying. The contrast and the surprise focus attention on the Samaritan. The clue to his behaviour is in the words 'he had compassion' (verse 33). This is not the Greek word meaning 'to suffer together with', but the one meaning 'to be moved with pity'.

**Attitude before Action**

The Good Samaritan is therefore (and here we move forward again in our laying bare of the roots of compassionate service) primarily *not about an action but about an attitude*. The Samaritan was so inwardly moved with pity that he had to do something about the man lying in need. This inwardness needs pondering. There are many reasons for serving others. Jesus highlights this one—an attitude which if present will issue in action.

We must not leave this clue yet. Another significant thing about it is that in the story a man's compassion for another broke down six centuries of hatred, built on events and nurtured in two cultures. It was more than an isolated incident. It was a signal, a breaching of the defences of prejudice, hate and suspicion. We need not look far for situations today where just such a signal is necessary in large numbers.

But this is the frustration of the story. How can one act like that? Is Jesus saying that any ordinary person is capable of so doing? It is an attractive solution, but one which does not accord with all the evidence. The word for 'he had compassion' is used in the Gospels only of Jesus, except on three occasions, each in a story told by Jesus to commend that particular attitude—here in the Good Samaritan, in the story of the Prodigal Son and in the story of the master who forgave his servant a huge debt. But only Jesus is actually recorded as having such an attitude. The likelihood is that the Lord is not saying that anyone can have such a compassion, but that in fact *no one can,* except by divine grace. It is a seminal attitude of the kingdom people, but they do not generate or sustain it. It is his gift.

**The Cost of Serving**
With the Good Smaritan we move on to yet another facet of compassionate service. *It is a costly commitment.* He risked his life, as well as his reputation, by his action. When we underline the importance of the Incarnation for our theme, we must not neglect the Death and Resurrection of Jesus. Involvement in humanity for the good of mankind was for Christ not only to risk life but to give it. John the Baptist was in this not only an announcer of Christ but a precursor of him, dying because he had spoken out about the immorality of Herod's behaviour (John 6:17–19). Jesus' commitment to the will of his Father, and through that to mankind in its need, could not be expressed in action to the full unless it knew no boundaries. The prayer in Gethsemane is the point at which this issue was finally settled. Commitment and cost in service go hand in hand.

**Old and New Testament Patterns**
Reference to the Cross and the Incarnation bring us to a cluster of issues, all related to the theme before us. The first concerns *the link with Old Testament patterns.* Apart from John the Baptist's testimony, Jesus himself is recorded as describing his ministry in terms borrowed from the prophets, Luke 4:18 (Isaiah 61:1) and Luke 7:22 (Isaiah 29:18–19; 35:5–6). The link between the nature and purposes of God on the one hand and the behaviour of his people on the other, supremely represented by Jesus Christ, is thus established as a 'kingdom pattern'.

**Deed and Word**

Two more delicate issues are raised by this connection. One concerns the relationship between *deed and word*. Both the Lukan passages quoted above, and their Old Testament counterparts, refer to proclamation *and* action. The question is whether these two elements are of equal importance. In Matthew's account of the early ministry of Jesus (Matthew 4:23) it seems that they were. 'And he went about all Galilee, teaching in the synagogues and preaching the gospel of the kingdom and healing every disease and every infirmity among the people.' Mark and Luke, however, both include the incident of Jesus' disciples finding him as he prayed alone (Mark 1:35–37) or the people finding him in a lonely place (Luke 4:42) and attempting to keep him in the one place. The setting in both accounts is of multiple healings. Yet his response is neither to stay nor to heal any more people there but to preach the good news in other places: 'for that is why I came out' (Mark 1:38); 'for I was sent for this purpose' (Luke 4:43). Is the significance here that the preaching is the main, central, normative activity in establishing the kingdom, and that the deeds of healing are signposts to the kingdom, of which the preaching is the entrance? Certainly our deeds, without interpretation, may not be understood. Without our ascription of our work to Jesus by our words, our deeds of kindness may direct gratitude in the wrong direction. The symbolic gesture requires the interpretative word.

**Physical and Spiritual**

The other delicate matter of interpretation concerns the *relationship of physical to spiritual* in the ministry of Jesus. It could be argued that the Gospel writers would not have understood such a distinction, or would not have considered it relevant to their story. But it is relevant for us since it has so divided the christian church. Mark 2:1–12 may provide us with a clue. In the story of the paralytic let down through the roof some scholars have discovered two separate accounts—a

saying and a healing—conflated together. Stylistic considerations enter into this question, alongside content. If the story
is taken as a whole, however, its significance harmonizes well
with the rest of the ministry of Jesus. Mark says that Jesus
posed to his critics the question whether it was easier to heal
the man's physical illness or to forgive his sins. Then, to
demonstrate that he could do the latter, he did the former.
Two points emerge from this story, and from much of the
Gospel material. One is *Jesus' concern for the whole of a
person*. His compassionate service did not select parts of a
person to help. Put like that the distinction sounds as ridicul-
ous as it in fact is! Yet, secondly, *the physical healings do
operate as signs*, or signposts, of the heart of the message,
which is forgiveness and inner renewal. This acceptance of
sinners, removing of the obstacle of their unworthiness, and
sending them off with a brand new beginning, is of the essence
of the kingdom. The physical restoration of the sick and the
possessed provided a powerful external pointer in that direction. Perhaps another way of expressing this is to remind
ourselves that the Incarnation culminated in the Death and
Resurrection.

**The Heart of the Matter**
Some roots remain uncovered by this survey. One hopes that
some, however, are clearly laid bare. Of these, the central
one, from which all others stem, is the nature and purpose of
God himself. Creation, Incarnation, Death and Resurrection
are all powerful expressions of this central feature. So is the
duty of the people of God to reflect the character of God. The
heart of the Gospel is God's offer of reconciliation to man in
his sinfulness and need; compassionate service is both a symbol and an expression of that offer.

# CHAPTER ELEVEN

# The Church as a Sign

THE miracle at Cana in Galilee is probably not a Methodist favourite. Turning water into wine has never been our strong point! Many of us would prefer a reverse procedure. But for that very reason we are in danger of missing a major point which John makes at the end of the story. 'This, the first of his signs, Jesus did at Cana in Galilee, and manifested his glory; and his disciples believed in him' (John 2:11). He sees the miracle as a sign—the first of many. His words are heavy with much greater meaning than that, however. In performing the signs Jesus 'manifested his glory'. And there was a result: 'The disciples believed'.

'Glory', in biblical usage, means 'the revealed presence'. The Israelites were often sustained by the glory of the Lord. John seems to be saying that when Jesus did what he did, there was a sense of the divine presence. The miracles did not prove anything, but they did indicate something. And part of their power to indicate lay in the sense of 'the glory'. It was this which led onlookers to believe.

Does this say something about the church today? Could it be that as God 'manifested glory' through the ministry of Christ, so today he wishes to 'manifest glory' through the body of Christ, the Church? It may be that a major reason for ineffectiveness in witness and dryness in worship (though these are by no means universal conditions in our churches) stem from a lack of 'the glory', the evidence of divine presence amongst us.

Jesus manifested his glory through the signs he performed. In what ways could the church today, and the lives of individual Christians, perform or be signs to manifest the glory?

We could be a sign that life is deep. Sadly, many of our fellows do not believe this to be the case. They see it as flat and rather shallow. Many are committed to a culture which is materialistic in basis. Things steadily encroach upon territory which used to belong to persons. Knowledge is reduced to that which can be proved. Reality is increasingly equated with observable phenomena. Steadily the hills and valleys of life are being flattened into an endless plain. Being is limited by what one can see, hear, taste, smell or touch. Beyond that little reality is expected.

Now the strange thing about the teaching of Jesus is that at first sight it would seem to confirm such an outlook. After all, the materials for his parables were all taken from the world of sight, sound and touch. Imagine a crowd of farmers hearing a speaker tell them that seeds put on rocks will not grow! Or that houses built on sand would not withstand the storm! Or that sons aren't always easy to manage! In one sense these stories—although most contained a surprise somewhere—could have been told by any of the hearers. At least, the materials for the parables were all a matter of common knowledge amongst the crowd.

Yet—and this is one of the great characteristics of Jesus' teaching—some heard much more than a fascinating and homely tale. It *was* possible to hear only the story, and probably to argue over which type of parable one preferred. But some returned to ask about the meaning. They had perceived that there was more here than simple story-telling. For them the parables opened widows on to heaven.

The parables certainly reveal something about Jesus himself. They also show the differences within the crowds, especially between those who earnestly sought the meaning and those who did not.

What we may often miss, however, is the fact that the parables say something about the ordinary, everyday objects, actions and events which compose the larger part of our lives. Probably all the crowd saw a sower. They were mostly sowers themselves at certain times of the year. But Jesus saw more than a sower at work. For him this familiar agricultural drama became the gateway to the mysterious and the transcendent. The perception of faith which he sought to communicate to his disciples included this. Families and farming, roads and houses, sons and servants, sheep and goats were all transcendent as in his hands they became pointers to the reality of God himself. The ordinary and everyday became the vehicle of the mysterious and the transcendent.

Have we Christians often reversed the process? Are we not often guilty of turning the mysterious and transcendent into the vehicle of the ordinary and everyday? It is so easy to trivialize the very being of God.

Take our worship, for example. One of my privileges as President of the Conference was to attend a Royal Garden Party at Buckingham Palace with my wife. There were many interesting people and things to see, but while the Queen was there she was the focal point of attention, and rightly so. Rightly so, because she is royalty. I found myself driving away after a marvellous day wondering whether the King of Kings is treated with such respect.

When our worship begins and our opening hymn is sung, do we really make it an offering of all of life as praise to our God and King? As the prayers are said, does one sense the quickening of the mood as each of us seeks to re-affirm our trust in our heavenly Father and our commitment to his way for us? Is the offering a token that everything we have and are is under his sovereign rule? And do we hear the word as those who are so grateful to be accepted by God in Christ and so glad to learn his will for us?

Worship like this celebrates life's hills and valleys.[1] Such experience of God in worship enables us to perceive his presence in the world through ordinary things. What is more, there is in such worship a sense of the glory. Unbelievers present witness ordinary, everyday people, but what is going on has a dimension which transcends the ordinary and everyday. In such circumstances 'the glory' can lead to 'belief'.

We may now turn from worship to consider work. It may seem a less likely scene of 'the glory'. Many years ago I heard the story of a young man who joined a firm of accountants. He said there was one of the firm with whom he hated to work. The reason was simple. This man started when they were paid to start, took no longer for breaks than was stipulated, and worked right up to the time when they were due to finish. It was all exhausting for the young man and most unwelcome. But when that young man, some time later, gave his life to Jesus Christ, it was because of the witness of the partner with whom he had originally so disliked working. As time went on he had discovered why this man applied himself to his work. It was because he saw it as an offering to God. The young man's name was Alan Redpath. He has since engaged in a renowned and effective ministry in many parts of the world, influencing the lives of millions of people. I don't know the name of that accountant, but it was 'the glory' in his working life which led a young man of enormous potential to believe.

When worship and work so conspire to demonstrate the depth of life, the church is being a sign of the kind God intends.

We are also called to be a sign of hope. It is a curious thing that in our welfare state there should be so many hopeless people. There are young folks, told to work hard to ensure a good career. They can see others who worked hard and

---

[1] I have tried to work out in more detail both the sources and the implications of this kind of worship in *God in the Gallery*, published by Epworth Press, 1975.

haven't got a career of any kind. Their parents tell them to prepare to take responsibility as the world is handed over to them. They look at it and wonder whether their parents wouldn't just keep it. It isn't worth inheriting. There are some hopeless young married couples, too. They married to solve their problems and in some cases have simply compounded them, and now they are trapped. There is hopelessness for some middle-aged couples, too. They have lived their lives for twenty or more years in the lives of their children. But now the children have gone away, trained, married, in their own homes. As a result some middle-aged couples are trying to recall whom they married and what they used to talk about. Then there is the most neglected group of all, the ageing unmarried person. Many have faithfully cared for their parents in the family home. But the parents are now dead, and the son or daughter lives on in a home whose every bit of furniture is a reminder. Many such single people wonder who in society cares for them, or where they are supposed to find fulfilling social life. And there are the old. I remember the searing story of the doctor examining an old man, who began to cry. The doctor assured him that he would suffer no hurt, to which the old man replied that he was crying, not because of the prospect of hurt, but because the doctor was the first person in six months to touch him. There is lots of hopelessness in our welfare state society.

I find myself at this point asking about the healing miracles of Jesus. Why did he heal the blind, deaf and dumb, lame and lepers? One reason was that they were the hopeless ones. It was for them that society could do so little. By his care for them Jesus declared that when the Kingdom of God comes in hopelessness goes out. The provision of hope was a sign of the glory.

At this point there is much of which the church in our country can be justly proud. Our involvement in voluntary caring associations in this country is probably without equal. Should all the Christians in Great Britain withdraw their voluntary service in society for six months, the nation might be greatly surprised. Secular as well as Christian bodies are highly dependent on Christian workers and supporters. The increasing use of church premises for such work is another pleasing aspect of the situation.

On two other levels however we have much less cause for satisfaction. One is our failure to discern or discover those who are hopeless but whose need is never registered with statutory or voluntary services. They are the hopeless whose real state is disguised by their being respectable, or intelligent, or otherwise able to mask their true state. Our churches, by and large, have few structures for becoming aware of such people. We also provide few openings (and the reputation to go with them) for people confidentially to reveal their need in a warm, caring atmosphere. Because of this weakness we miss much spiritual need to which we could minister.

The other level about which we are rightly dissatisfied is that of the structures of political power in our nation. The frustration felt by many Christians in times of industrial unrest leads for increasing calls to church leaders to 'speak out'. No one belives that such 'speaking out' will solve the problem or save the situation. It often complicates it further. The industrial and political situation is currently much too complex to be so solved. Only those engaged at the heart of it are likely to produce solutions. Maybe this is where much of the Christian frustration comes from. We are not, as Christians, largely represented at the places where the complexity, risk and power are greatest. We are better at distributing charity than at battling for justice. I do not believe that the Kingdom of God will be established by political action. Nor do I think we will ever get the society we dream of till all men and women are born again by God's Spirit through faith in Christ. But I do believe that every Christian should be concerned for a better world, for the establishing of justice on earth, and for a situation where every human being is able to live a fully human life. We will never fulfil that obligation if we all steer clear of political responsibility. Yet at present Christians in politics are somewhat lonely and isolated people because so few others are in the sub-structures below them.

It should be as natural for a Christian to feel called by God to a life in politics for Christ's sake, as to a life in the ordained ministry for the same reason. But this will only happen as within our fellowships and church activities we are increasingly concerned with understanding and caring about the political, industrial and social situation in our land, as well as the spiritual and moral climate. I could wish that every Christian belonged to a group for Bible study, discovering basic principles and applying them to daily life; *and* to a group which study modern problems, seeking to work through the problems to distinctively Christian solutions. The combination of these two activities in every church might well ignite a flame of considerable proportion. Our concern for the hopeless would be quickened and expressed, too, so that 'the glory' might be manifested.

In our land there is a great need for genuine grounds of hope to be demonstrated. Conversely, within the church there appears to be a growing Spirit of hope. We survived the deep heart-searchings of the sixties. We have evened out in the seventies. There is a sense of hope for the eighties. But it must be well grounded in reality, and expressed in our actions if people are to perceive the glory and believe.

Next we should be a sign to the suffering. It is a sobering thought that, one way or another, the suffering are probably half the world's population at any given time. If we think of the hungry and homeless, the ill and the neglected, the bereaved and the under-privileged, the figure is enormous. What have we to say to the suffering? And if we have nothing of weight to say to them, ought we to say anything to anyone?

He would be a fool who claimed to be able to solve the problem of suffering. He is equally a fool who seeks to offer help in trite statements: 'you can always find someone worse off than yourself', 'the first year is always the worst', 'smile,

Jesus loves you'. Worst of all 'I understand how you feel'. In the presence of the suffering those things are surely best left unsaid.

Yet there is one thing to be said. At the Bradford Methodist Conference in 1978 one of the District Chairmen, the Reverend Christopher Hughes Smith, was invited, with others, to say briefly how he perceived God to be at work in his life. He reported on his recent visit to Ireland and concluded 'I have to say that I can see no solution to the problems of that country'. He then added 'I am grateful that we have a faith with death and resurrection at its centre'.

I believe that he had in that short time touched on the nub of the matter. The heart of our *good* news is the most undeserved death in human history. The crucifying of the only truly good man the world has ever known—the Son of God—is unparalleled in history. At the centre of our message is therefore the affirmation that God understands suffering. Through Christ he declares himself at one with our suffering and identifying himself with us in it. There *is* one who stands beside us in our suffering, one who has plumbed the depths of all sufferings in his own experience of it in Christ. There *is* something there which is worth saying, for it links us to the reality of the divine sympathy and comfort.

What is more, since Christ's death was followed by resurrection (which is why we have good news at all) there is the possibility that even out of tragedy and suffering some good may come. We are directed away from the question 'why did it happen?', a question unlikely to be satisfactorily answered in many cases. We are pointed towards the question 'what will the result be?' In answering this question we have a part to play, and drawing upon the comfort and power of God there is a hope of good even out of tragedy.

I stood in the bedroom of one of our ministers who was dying. He told me of one dark night when he felt the power of evil against him. He felt something of what the Lord must have gone through in the agony of the Cross. All through that night, he told me, he held his wife's hand and repeated some words of John Wesley, 'The best of all is, God is with us'. I felt how deeply God was in that experience and in that room. We were facing suffering at the foot of the Cross in sure and certain hope of the Resurrection, and the glory was manifested. In that situation it was not difficult to believe.

Another sign we are meant to provide is that of forgiveness. One of the sad developments of this century has been the passing out of the hands of the church of care for those who feel guilty. This is not to mount an attack on psychiatric medical practice. I have no competence to do so in any case. But the movement away from church care of such people has had two results in many cases. The first is that much advice to the guilty appears to assume that there is no need to feel guilty. It is all somehow the fault of others and of our circumstances. One thinks of the schoolboy, as his father was reading his very poor end-of-term report, asking: 'Dad, what do you think my trouble is, heredity or environment?'! Now one realizes that there are those who suffer from a guilt complex, and who need a cure for it. But most of us ought really to face up to our genuine responsibility for anything less than the best, and to see that our guilt in that context is well-placed. It is not helpful advice which tells us that we are not really responsible. In the end that will undermine us as human beings.

The other result of a secular, medical approach to the problem of guilt is that it omits the most important aspect, from the Christian point of view. We are justified in feeling guilty about our wrongs against our fellow men and women. But our guilt is greater than we acknowledge if we see it only at that level. The Christian view of our guilt is that it is greatest before God, not man. Every offence committed, every good deed omitted, is supremely a wrong before God. We do well to feel guilty—for we are—and before the very highest court of judgment. We help no one by disguising this insight into our true state. Neither the human psyche nor the state of humanity are helped by such masking of the truth. Of course we do not wish to leave ourselves or others there. The great joy of our good news is that in Christ we are forgiven. Our message declares it and our sacraments symbolize it. In a culture where meritocracy exhausts the successful and eliminates the rest we can know that God will accept us, not because of who we are or what we have achieved, but because his love is like that. In a world where more and more information about wider and wider areas of life tinges every enjoyment with guilt about the conditions of others, we can know that we are forgiven. Yet it is never cheap grace. We are unworthy to be accepted, but he who accepts us in Christ seeks to make our lives increasingly worthy. We are forgiven in Christ, but he who forgives will enable us to conquer those elements in our lives which cause us to be guilty. He receives us as we are but he does not leave us as we are.

I heard Miss Pauline Webb recount, at the 1978 Anniversary of the Manchester Mission, some of her experiences when visiting the West Indies. She described an old lady walking down the mountains for ten hours, carrying her shoes lest she should scratch them. The reason for such special effort became apparent when, in the Holy Communion service, the congregation were invited forward to receive bread and wine. Now the old lady had her shoes on. She walked down the aisle with all the regal bearing of a Queen, but to receive bread and wine, the tokens of divine forgiveness and acceptance—the extravagant generosity of divine grace. Then, her purpose achieved, she set off up the mountains again. That story took us to the very heart of the gospel—forgiveness, acceptance and renewal through Christ.

In our proper concern about church structures, liturgical form, evangelistic method and social service, could it be that we have overlaid the central thrust of our message? Our world certainly needs to learn more about grace. But we are dependent on it too, for our own spiritual life and for a discovery of our unity as Christians. Perhaps we Christians would forgive one another more freely and deeply if we lived closer to this truth. Where forgiveness in Christ is offered and received, there is a sign to manifest the glory, and people are helped to believe.

There is a fifth sign—the sign of integrity. By this I mean not simply—or principally—that we should be trustworthy people; those who keep their word. I mean something much deeper. Christian integrity is to live by what we believe and affirm. Helmut Thielicke wrote of a loss of credibility between pew and pulpit. It was not that the congregation rejected the truth of the message proclaimed week by week. It was rather that the preacher didn't 'live in the house of his faith'. There was a fear that what the preacher lived by on Monday was not the message he had proclaimed on Sunday.

Of course it would take many books to expound what it means to live by one's faith. But we can take one major motif from the New Testament and look at the Christian life from that point of view. Death and resurrection is one such theme.

New Testament writers do not exhort their readers simply to 'believe in' the Cross of Christ, or his death and resurrection. Their emphasis is not so much upon believing it alone as upon experiencing it by faith. Thus Jesus is recorded as telling his disciples to 'take up' *their* crosses and follow him.[2] Paul sees the Christian as buried with Christ and raised with him.[3] The argument is that we not only accept the fact and meaning of Christ's death and resurrection. We are actually associated with them, incorporated into them. What he did in dying and rising was done for us. By faith we count ourselves in on his death and resurrection because God so counts us in.[4] Put another way it means that whatever Christ died to we count ourselves dead to, and whatever he rose to we are risen to.[5]

It is as we enter into this incorporation that we experience the power of Christ's death and resurrection. We may see an

[2] Matthew 16:24; Mark 8:34; Luke 14:27.
[3] Romans 6:4–11; Colossians 2:11–15, 3:1–4.
[4] Corinthians 5:14–15.
[5] See Romans 6 again.

illustration in flying. The essential unlikelihood of getting all those people, together with luggage, freight and machinery, off the ground and then propelling them through the air, is extremely high. At least it feels so as one sits in the full plane on the ground. It would be very strange indeed, however, if before the flight the Captain advised passengers to lift mats at their feet, revealing holes in the floor of the plane, and asked the passengers to put their legs through the holes till their feet touched the ground. Even stranger to be told all to run together on instruction, and at the end of the runway to jump in unison! In fact quite the opposite happens. You fasten your seat-belt, feel the plane quiver as the engines build up power, then find yourself borne high into the air by that same power. You fly by committing yourself to a power greater than yours, and by risking your life to it.

To live as a sign of integrity is something like that. It is to recognize that death and resurrection with Christ is a way into the heart of Christian experience. It is to commit oneself to the implications and to live by it. It is to experience the power thus made available in the risen Christ. It is to be a sign by which the glory is manifested.

# CHAPTER TWELVE

# Grace and Mission

*Sermon at the Dedication Service of the*
*Nationwide Initiative in Evangelism,*
*Lambeth Palace, London*
*22 January 1979*

THIS is an historic occasion for us all. Many of us have previously worshipped with some others who are here, but never before have we all worshipped together in this way. Indeed, at a national level such a service has probably never taken place in England before. The groups of christians we represent have usually found it much easier to be apart than together. We are right to feel a certain awe—and expectancy—on such an occasion.

Of course it has to be clearly stated that we represent varying degrees of commitment to the Nationwide Initiative in Evangelism for which we have come to pray. But all are here to commend the Initiative to God, and to do so together. By this single act we cross boundaries and barriers which have kept us apart for centuries. Few of us can fail to be deeply moved by the privilege of sharing such an experience.

I hope that the nation at large will notice that on a day

marked by strikes—themselves symbols of unreconciliation and distrust—the leaders of most of the Christians in England took a decisive step towards deeper reconciliation and stronger trust within the one body of Christ, and that we have done so not for our own sakes. but for those who do not yet believe in Jesus Christ as Saviour and Lord. Maybe this service is itself an effective sign of what the Initiative is about; sharing with one another what it means to us to be Christians and committing ourselves to make the Good News known as widely as possible in our land.

A good starting point in the Bible is therefore Antioch where, Luke tells us in Acts 11:26, 'the disciples were for the first time called Christians'. It seems appropriate to match a first time with a first time. Some of the ingredients of Luke's account have a peculiar relevance for us today.

Antioch provided no more fertile soil for Christian growth than does modern England. It was large; the third largest city in the Roman Empire. It was prosperous. It had a reputation for immorality and it was greatly influenced by the worship of other gods, in particular Artemis and Apollo. It was the major centre for Jews dispersed from their own country.

To this unlikely spot Barnabas was sent from the church in Jerusalem because of the disturbing news that non-Jews were claiming to be Christian believers—a shocking departure. We may find helpful guide-lines in the situation Barnabas faced and in the responses he made.

1. The clue to the puzzle is *the operation of divine grace*. Barnabas (investigating the situation) 'saw the grace of God' (Acts 11:23). He went to examine a series of events and a group of people, in order to determine their authenticity or inauthenticity. What he found were the signs of God's free forgiving activity through Jesus Christ—the same as he and the other Christian leaders had experienced. In Antioch, as in Jerusalem, people had found new life in Christ. That one group were Gentiles and the other Jews made no difference to the origin of their new and transforming experience. The

plant was in some respects different: the root was the same. I am conscious of a certain resonance between that situation and ours. Each of us is the inheritor of a tradition which is precious to us. We know that there are other traditions, many of them represented here. We may be forgiven for feeling that ours cuts the straightest path back to the foundational demonstration of God's grace in the life, death and resurrection of Jesus Christ. We may feel that our way is not only straighter, but also clearer, purer and fuller than any other! And we would wish to claim its present experience of divine grace too. Yet however superior (albeit humbly!) we feel our tradition to be, would any of us wish to claim that any other person here, or any other group represented here, is alien to that grace or does not grow from the same root? Whatever our differences we all owe our standing as Christians to God's free undeserved favour in Christ, ministered to us through the Holy Spirit, interpreted for us in Holy Scriptures and preserved for us within the life of the Church.

Our willingness to affirm and live within this truth is directly related to our evangelism. If there is any one realization needed by our society more than any other, it is the meaning of grace. In these past few weeks our political and industrial world has been dominated by incessant clamour on every side concerning rights. Discussions about justice are diverted into wrangling about law. The tenor of our national life lacks the note of graciousness typified by God's giving of his life to us in Christ. The parable of the Vineyard labourers was never in my judgment intended to be a manifesto for management–labour relations. But it speaks of a graciousness to others without which no relationship—industrial or any other—can hope to achieve the goals of justice and human fulfilment. Have we not a word to speak to the nation at this moment about grace? Ought not more of our resources of time, money and personnel to be allocated to the task of making God's grace in Christ known in our society? But we may only speak it as our own lives and relationships reflect it.

It is at this point that 'convergence' offers us a better model than 'consensus' as a way forward. 'Consensus' is about establishing areas of doctrinal agreement before any advance can be made. It is almost inevitably connected to a static view of doctrine. It proceeds by excluding the variously unacceptable points and softening the sharp edges of the rest. The result is often minimal and ineffective. By contrast 'convergence' is about advancing together in a discovery of what we have in common and acting accordingly. It is mobile, involving mutual movement towards the centre. It does not require overall agreement on every point, but only action in relation to those points which are mutually agreed. The degree of convergence revealed in the Lausanne, Nairobi and Evangelii Nuntiandi Reports is enough to give hope in the specific area of evangelism. *And the centre to which we move together is the grace of God, revealed in Jesus Christ.* It is the centre both of our church life and of our witness in the world. The Initiative is committed to keeping the convergence debate going and to extending its scope to include local groups of Christians.

2. If this is to succeed at all, however, we need *people who can perceive God's grace when they see it.* This is the ability which Barnabas revealed, and which broke the potential log-jam in the early Church. Successive movements in the life of the Christian Church in this century have had a similar effect on the log-jam of our denominational relationships. Missionary enterprise, the biblical theology movement, commitment to social and political involvement, liturgical commissions, charismatic experience and the more recent renewal of evangelistic concern have all caused people to step across denominational boundaries in the interests of some other common bond.

The question we now face is whether we can find ways of crossing the newly-formed boundaries also. We shall face the same problems as our more recent and our original predecessors. It is safer and easier to have groups or individuals whose word and action we always (or mostly) trust, and conversely those whom we never (or rarely) heed. Can we bear to expose ourselves to the simple question 'Is this the grace of God?', wherever I perceive it? To put it another way, are we able to see the difference between what comes out of *our* stable, and what comes from *the original* stable, as the basic test? Have we the courage to affirm our fellow Christians, with whom we disagree, as nevertheless exhibiting the fruit of the Spirit in the life of grace? This is not to neglect questions of truth about doctrine or of order in the life of the Church. But it is to put them into their proper perspective. Without the priority of God's grace offered to us in Christ neither questions of theological truth nor issues of church order are relevant. The willing acceptance of divine grace brings us near enough to one another to discuss truth and order And divine grace at the heart of our evangelism will show the folly of separating service and proclamation as though one could properly exist without the other. Grace gives itself to the need of others, whatever their need—and to their entire need, however varied or extensive it may be. God's grace is for the whole of a person and the whole of a society. This is why the Nationwide Initiative in Evangelism must help Christians at the local level to ask serious questions about the nature of our society, the significance of its concerns, and the appropriate meeting points between these concerns and the insights we gain from the Christian gospel. We must try to understand our society as well as our message if the two are to meet effectively. Our roles in the Church and outside it then become matters of prime concern, and our judgments about them must be based upon accurate evidence. That we view these roles differently may well be a sign of our richness rather than a reason for division.

3. A third requirement of us is *to enable others to play their part within the atmosphere of divine grace*. Barnabas saw the evidence of grace, exhorted the converts to continue in it (verse 23), but knew that he was not the man to continue that work. He did believe, however, that God had a man ready,

Saul of Tarsus. Barnabas made it possible for Antioch to benefit from Paul's ministry, and for Paul to fulfil his calling according to the training, gifts and insights he had received.

Part of our weakness today stems from our failure to realize how much resource God has given to his Church in our country. This Initiative should help the churches locally, and Christians individually, to assess both their tasks and their resources in evangelism. It should encourage imaginative new insights and methods as well as renewing traditional ones. It should enable the latent evangelistic energy of the local churches to be harnessed effectively in each place where Christians are. And it should encourage Christians to engage in this task together. To some extent the success of the Initiative depends upon the willingness of local Christians to discover and apply adequate resources in effective evangelism and by our capacity to help them to do so.

But what chance have we of achieving all, or any, of this? Even assuming that it is part of what God is doing in his Church today, we ourselves still carry heavy responsibility. Luke tells us that Barnabas was able to play his part adequately because he was 'a good man, full of the Holy Spirit and of faith'. We meet today to ask God to renew in us, and in all his people, those qualities of goodness, fullness of the Holy Spirit, and faith by which we may be enabled to play our parts too. No one can predict the results of the Initiative we take today. We can all pray that by God's grace they will be worthy and lasting. And we can commit ourselves to make them so.

CHAPTER THIRTEEN

# The Rhythm of Worship and Mission

*Sermon at the Festival of the Open Door,*
*Wesley's Chapel, City Road, London*
*5 November 1978*

LAST Wednesday this Chapel was full to capacity three times over. We were reopening it, after extensive renovations, two hundred years to the day since John Wesley, Methodism's founder, had opened it. Her Majesty the Queen attended the first of the services, His Royal Highness Prince Philip read a lesson, and leaders of other Christian churches were present. We also had the representatives of the Methodist family from all round the world, a family numbering some twenty millions. It was a memorable day for Methodists.

Today we get down to business with the hard question 'What is the point of it all?' Why spend any money restoring a church? Of course its historical significance is obvious. For millions of Methodists this Chapel is their spiritual home. To restore it is to secure our heritage. But wouldn't a museum do that just as well? What difference does it make to call it a chapel?

In one sense we answer that question today by combining in

this service the Festival of the Open Door and the Lord's Supper, Holy Communion.

The Festival of the Open Door will also be shared by millions of Methodists around the world. At the end of the service we shall open our doors in a symbolic action. In so doing we make it plain that all are welcome to join us in worship here at any time. We also commit ourselves to go out into everyday life to serve others and to make known the good news about Jesus Christ.

At this point the imagery of the door has great significance for Christians. As we heard in our lesson, Jesus spoke of himself as the door. The picture is one of the shepherd guarding his sheep. It was apparently the practice of some shepherds in Palestine to place themselves in the gap which was the gateway of the sheepfold. Thus they were literally the door. As Jesus said, the sheep went in and out to find pasture by way of the Shepherd.

Now the opening of the doors for entry and exit begins to have much more meaning. We are talking about going out into daily life by way of Christ, and returning here again by way of Christ. But what does it mean?

It involves seeing the world, and life in the world, as the place where God's presence can be known. Jesus and his disciples probably all saw a sower sowing seed. But he saw something more then they did. Perhaps they all saw men building houses, bridesmaids at a wedding, rich men with their servants. These were the stuff of ordinary life. But Jesus saw in them pictures of the way God deals with his world. He took the ordinary, everyday events of life and turned them into vehicles to bring us to the experience of mystery and transcendence.

To begin to look at life like that can make all the difference. It means to affirm that the world is God's creation and that it is full of events and experiences which can make us aware of his presence. The birth of a baby, the presence of a couple in love, the awesomeness of a landscape, the beauty of a piece of music, the poignancy of deep friendship, the receipt of unexpected kindness, and even the depth of sorrow can be such events and experiences. They are capable of natural explanations and yet they seem to possess a depth which is unsatisfied by purely natural descriptions. They cannot *prove* God's existence, but they can be signposts, put up by the Creator to indicate his presence within his creation; signals that life is deep and meaningful, and that at its heart is the being of God himself.

For those who see the world like this, the doors of the Chapel are open not as an option but as a necessity. Here, with others of his people, we celebrate life as God's gift. The hour we spend in worship dedicates all our time to him. Our prayers mark all life as depending upon his grace. Our hymns establish the hope that every part of life will be worthy of him. Our gifts are a signal that all we possess is at his disposal. Our hearing the word and receiving the Sacraments reflect our desire that all of life be directed by his love and truth. Thus worship and fellowship are at the centre of daily life, not separate entities from it.

Yet Christ did more than point to God's presence in the world. He also showed what a perfected human life could be like. The mystery of his nature as God and Man is not easily explained. But its effect upon those he met is described in the New Testament. People who took him seriously had either to get rid of him or to face the ugly contrast between his life and theirs. The very presence of this perfectly good life brought crisis; a decision for or against the good—judgment.

To go out through those doors by way of Christ is to go out recognizing that we are not able to live up to his standards. The potential of a world sustained by the very being of God is not realized because of our failure to live by what we perceive of its possibilities. What is worse, our failure is often wilful and culpable. Our corporate failures marked out by war, starvation, underprivilege and pollution, are reflections of our individual failures in relationships, in caring for others, in controlling our pride or keeping ourselves pure. And there, written into history, is the life of Jesus Christ—a goal of perfection and a reminder of our inadequacy.

Such realization will again bring us through the doors into church, not only to affirm life and its possibilities but also to confess sin and its consequences. The common picture of church-goers as the club of respectable citizens has a strange irony about it! Our view of ourselves would be somewhat different. We come here because here, before God and with his people, we not only offer all of life to him again. We also know what it is to be forgiven and accepted.

At the very heart of this perfected life of Jesus Christ are his death and resurrection. To go out and come in by way of him is to do so knowing that his self-giving love in death and resurrection both reflects God's love and opens up for us a way into it. By dying and rising he has broken the inevitability of failure and misery as the pattern of human existence. Here in our worship we acknowledge our faults, we claim God's grace in word and sacrament, we hear the assurance, as we have done in our service today, 'In Christ you are forgiven'. In this place we discover the deep mystery of God's grace. Unworthy though we are, we are welcomed. We are accepted.

There is a third implication of going in and out by way of Christ. It is that we do not go or return alone. We go as witnesses—witnesses to the presence of God in his world and witnesses to the fact that those who confess their failure and offer their lives are both forgiven and transformed by the mystery of new birth. We go as those whose perception of God is being deepened and whose life is being changed. And God both precedes us and goes with us. He precedes us in that he is at work in his world all the time. He goes with us in that our message *about* Christ, and our lives *reflecting* Christ, are the clue to others concerning what God is doing in their lives. In that sense we both discern Christ *in* the world *and* proclaim Christ *to* the world; and he whom we proclaim is with us, as he promised, 'I am with you to the end of the ages'.

The next question is 'Will we be able to achieve what we intend?' Will the worship we offer be worthy of God? Will our service and witness in the world be winsome and clear? We know how easy it is to fail. Have we any chance of succeeding?

Our Holy Communion Service will remind us of one answer to that question. We do not keep the Christian faith up; it keeps us up. We do not support Christ; he supports us. As we receive bread and wine in this sacramental act we remember that Christ does not only call people to his service. He also sustains them in it.

John Wesley, after whom this Chapel is named, used different language to describe the things we have considered this morning. He believed in the hidden operation of God the Spirit drawing men and women to God midst the variety of ordinary experiences. This he called prevenient grace—grace which goes ahead. He saw the heart of Christ's death on the Cross as the offer of pardon for sin. He laid upon his followers the responsibility of making the good news known, by their deeds and by their words. And it was all undergirded by his often celebrated words, 'The best of all is, God is with us'. As we take bread and wine, as we open our doors in this special festival, let those words ring in our ears and resound in our lives. 'The best of all is, God is with us.'